Leading Impact Teams

Leading Impact Teams

Building a Culture of Efficacy

Paul Bloomberg

Barb Pitchford

Foreword by John Hattie

CORWIN

A SAGE Publishing Company

FOR INFORMATION:

Corwin

A SAGE Company

2455 Teller Road

Thousand Oaks, California 91320

(800) 233-9936

www.corwin.com

SAGE Publications Ltd.

1 Oliver's Yard

55 City Road

London EC1Y 1SP

United Kingdom

SAGE Publications India Pvt. Ltd.

B 1/I 1 Mohan Cooperative Industrial Area

Mathura Road, New Delhi 110 044

India

SAGE Publications Asia-Pacific Pte. Ltd.

3 Church Street

#10-04 Samsung Hub

Singapore 049483

Printed in the United States of America

ISBN 978-1-5063-2267-4

Program Director: Dan Alpert

Senior Associate Editor: Kimberly Greenberg

Editorial Assistant: Katie Crilley

Production Editor: Amy Schroller

Copy Editor: Deanna Noga

Typesetter: C&M Digitals (P) Ltd.

Proofreader: Sally Jaskold

Indexer: Karen Wiley

Cover Designer: Michael Dubowe

Marketing Manager: Charline Maher

This book is printed on acid-free paper.

19 20 21 22 11 10 9 8 7 6

Contents

Foreword

The latest hot topic among educators is teacher collective efficacy—that is, teachers working together to build the confidence that they can get all students to advance in learning. The effect size from the recent work by Rachel Eells (2011) places it among the most powerful influences on student learning (at d = 1.57). Teachers' collective efficacy is quite specific—it is teachers working together, building mindsets that all students can make appreciable progress, and then reinforcing these efficacy beliefs with evidence that students do indeed learn by these teachers "causing learning."

Leading Impact Teams: Building a Culture of Efficacy combines some of the best innovations from the last decade to ensure a focus on changing the learning lives of students. Like all good cake recipes, it is not just the ingredients but also the way they are combined that matters the most—and the tender, loving care illustrated throughout these chapters as to the combination is the key to this book's success: building a culture of efficacy in leaders, teachers, and students based on developing impact teams.

To enable teachers to understand, to build confidence in growth, and then to feed this growth with evidence of actual student growth typically involves a determined, focused, and knowledgeable leader. It needs an instructional leader who finds the space, resources, and time for this to occur, to ensure its implementation, and to evaluate its impact. These are the themes outlined in this book—how to LEAD teams that have IMPACT by building TEAMS to have a CULTURE OF EFFICACY. At last we move past collecting data and then forming teams (or professional learning communities) to the more important working together to interpret the impact of our teaching on each and every student's learning. This interpreting is the core notion of clinical practice in most professions. This is contrary to the usual life of teachers—working alone (but often sitting together working alone), the classroom door closed, the discussion about their impact reserved for their anecdotes and selective memory of what worked, and designing pre-specific activities to engage students and keep them on target until the bell goes. Instead, the focus is more on the consequences of the activities, the magnitude of the growth, the working together to maximize impact, and the sharing of these debates among colleagues (including with the students).

Such a method requires high levels of trust, a notion often referenced in the book. In some of my team's work this building of trust can take months before we can move to collaborate teams to develop high levels of efficacy. Teachers and schools have been so bashed in the past decades that they are appropriately nervous about sharing data and evidence—it has been so often used against them. Instead, this book is premised on the notion that there is considerable success all around us in schools, and it asks how we can reliably identify this expertise, use it in impact teams, and share and develop the expertise. Such scaling up of success is the ever-charging battery in this process.

This book asks us all to move away from setting up another team, yet again having another look at data, and arranging another professional learning community. Instead it has a laser focus on the purposes of these communities—to maximize impact on student learning *together*. This means that we need to ask about the evidence to make these impact decisions—and here is the place of formative evaluation of student work, both helping the students to know where to go next and helping the teachers best guide them in the next phase of the progression toward meeting the success criteria.

Of course, I am delighted they use my synthesis of meta-analyses to help inform their claims in this book. The reason it took me 15 years to write the first Visible Learning book related to creating the story underlying the data is that gathering the data was the easier part, and interpreting it and checking that others understood my interpretation was the hard part. Similarly, throughout this book Bloomberg and Pitchford emphasize the interpretation, show how teams help shape these interpretations, and discuss how teams provide an opportunity for checking the veracity and impact of these interpretations. It is the building of the story about the data that is more critical than the data (not that the data should be other than reliable and valid)—but it is the skill of interpreting the evidence that makes this book successful, in the same way that the skill of interpreting the evidence about student learning makes the teachers successful.

My theme is about maximizing impact, and this means a robust discussion in any education setting about what we collectively understand by this term. Progression in learning should not be left to the particular beliefs of any one teacher, but a sense of progress should come from all that students encounter in a school. To me, it is more than scores on tests, it involves inviting students to want to participate in learning, it involves a joy of learning and taking on challenges, it is knowing when one is successful in learning, and it is knowing sufficient strategies to be able to choose among them to trial pathways to solutions. It does involve attaining precious knowledge, and I am continually reminded of Michael Young's claims that such attainment includes providing students with knowledge they would not get if they did not come to school.

Maximizing this impact involves teachers learning from students about their impact—and this is the heart of formative evaluation, which in turn is the substance of collaborative inquiry among teacher teams. This demands that instructional leaders hone the purpose, build the trust, and ensure the communication. This demands high levels of social sensitivity to others, respect for evidence, and beliefs that all can cause learning. All these are the core of Bloomberg and Pitchford's Impact Team Model.

They outline the what, why, and how aspects of building these teams, continually feeding the team back with evidence of its impact and reflections on whether this impact is sufficient for the time and energies imparted, which ensures that there is evidence put into action. Finally, a core purpose for impact teams—and it is a virtuous circle—that the evidence and analysis lead to action feeds back in the team, and the students are the beneficiaries. Oh, so are the teachers, as one of the major reasons we are in this business of education is to have an impact on all students!

—John Hattie

Acknowledgments

When we were asked whom to acknowledge for this book, the first thing that came out of both of our mouths was "our partner districts, schools, teachers, and students!" This book simply would not have happened without the many thought partners we have worked with over the past several years who were willing to take risks with us and who believe what we believe in. We are deeply indebted to the students, the teachers, and the leaders who worked with us to develop the Impact Team Model.

Thank you to the following thought partners:

- Louise Alfano, Principal, PS 112, District 20, and her team of dedicated teachers and leaders
- Lisa Arcuri, Principal, PS 5, District 20, NYC DOE, and her team of teachers
- Eric Bloomberg, former Learning Network Specialist, The Core Collaborative, and Paul's nephew
- John Boyle, Principal, Totten Intermediate School, District 31, NYC DOE, and his dedicated team of teachers and leaders
- Mark Brewer and Lisa Aguerria Lewis, Assistant Superintendents, PVUSD, Watsonville, CA
- Christine Chavez, Principal, PS 45, District 31, NYC DOE, and her team of dedicated teachers and assistant principals
- The Core Collaborative—all of the partner consultants, San Diego, CA
- Alan Daly, Professor and Chair, Department of Education Studies at University of California, San Diego
- East Central BOCES, Limon, CO: Don Anderson, Sharon Daxton-Vorce, Jodi Church, Megan Donnellon, Pam Pekarek, Anita Burns, and Mitzi Swiatkowski, and all the cooperating districts and schools in the BOCES

- Melissa Garofalo, Principal, PS 45, District 31, NYC DOE, and her team of dedicated teachers
- Jodi Gronvold, Principal, Reeds Spring Intermediate School, Reeds Spring School District, Reeds Spring, MO
- Tom Hilz and Monica Cesarello and their team at Macquiddy Elementary in PVUSD, Watsonville, CA
- Joplin School District, Joplin, MO: principals, teacher leaders, and district office leadership
- Anthony Lodico, Superintendent of District 31, NYC DOE and his team: Vincenza Gallassio, Joe Zaza, Lorrie Brown, Christine Loughlin
- Lyons Township High School Administration in La Grange, IL, with special thanks to the first 10 Model Impact Teams and Virginia Condon, Michelle Harbin, and James Milkert for recording their efforts implementing the EAA Classroom Protocol
- Deanna Marco, Principal, PS 9, District 31, NYC DOE, and her team of dedicated teachers and leaders
- Kathy Mathison, former Director of Professional Development, Lamar Independent Consolidated School District, Rosenberg, TX
- Mark Melendez, Principal, Hutchinson Elementary School, Lamar Independent School District, Rosenberg, TX
- Dawn Minutelli and her team at Sunnyside Elementary, Chula Vista Elementary School District in Chula Vista, CA
- Julie Munn and her team at Kelsey Norman Elementary, Joplin Schools, Joplin, MO
- Chris Ogno, Principal, PS 247, District 20, NYC DOE, and his team of dedicated assistant principals and teachers
- Heidi Paul, Principal, Bell Elementary School, Lake Washington School District, Redmond, WA
- Kelly Pease, Director of School Support, ELL/Safety Net, Lake Washington School District, Redmond, WA
- Susan Perez, Assistant Superintendent, and her team at Pajaro Valley Unified School District, Watsonville, CA
- Anne Plancher, Deputy Director of Teaching and Learning, and her team at the Staten Island Borough Field Support Center, NYC DOE
- Guillermo Ramos and Claudia Monasterio, and their team at Hall District Elementary in PVUSD, Watsonville, CA
- Santa Cruz City Schools, Santa Cruz, CA
- Bill Schneden, Executive Director, Davenport Community Schools, Davenport, Iowa
- Sarah Stevens, Director of Professional Learning, The Core Collaborative, and the former Director of Curriculum and Instruction, Joplin School District

- Chris Templeton, Assistant Superintendent, Reeds Spring School District, Reeds Spring, MO
- Annette Villerot, Assistant Superintendent of Curriculum and Instruction, Pflugerville ISD, Pflugerville, TX, and her curriculum team

Thank you to Corwin, and especially to Kristin Anderson for taking a chance on us. In one conversation, she framed our message and strengthened our work around our profound belief—that when teachers believe they can make a difference for ALL students, they actually do!

Finally, we would like to say a special thank you to John Hattie, who guided our work and who wrote the Foreword to this book. His research has inspired us to truly make a difference!

From Barb Pitchford

We didn't choose each other, the work chose for us. However it happened, I am thankful for the most talented and brilliant writing partner on the planet. I now realize that having a writing partner is a bit like a marriage—many challenges, non-stop learning, and so cool to have someone to share the successes with.

Special thanks to my children, Molly and Scott, who have always hung in there with me even when they had to spend many a long day at school with me.

And to my family and friends who know and understand my passion for the work and are there to cheer me on but also to remind me about this thing called "balance"—to go for a hike or ride my horse.

And to the many teachers who have worked with me over the years – you have been my teachers!

From Paul Bloomberg

I am very grateful for my amazing writing partner and confidante, Barb Pitchford. We have been on quite a journey over the past 5 years and tried to ensure that students remained at the center while writing this book and developing the Impact Team Model. There is no greater gift than when students take ownership of their learning, mistakes and all.

A special thanks to:

My parents, Jon and Marilyn Bloomberg, who always kept me and my brothers focused on setting goals and being mindful of others and urged us to make a "dent in the world" by making a difference in the lives of other people.

Dean Christopher and John Nichol—I was lucky to have teachers who believed in me throughout my journey as a student and teacher; these amazing people taught me the benefit of giving back to the communities they served, and they always put their heart in everything they did.

Talonya, one of my many students—she taught me how to truly partner with students, and now we have been best friends for over 20 years.

Alex and Taylor, my sons, have taught me how important it is for students to take ownership of their learning.

Mimi Aronson, my hero, taught me to always trust students to lead the way, and they never have let me down.

Tony, my husband, believes in this work as much as Barb and I do, and we love him for his unwavering support, his sacrifice, and dedication to making a difference in the lives of ALL students.

Publisher's Acknowledgments

Corwin gratefully acknowledges the contributions of the following reviewers:

Susan Kessler, EdD
Executive Principal
Hunters Lane High School—
    Metropolitan Nashville
    Public Schools
Nashville, TN

Roberto Pamas
Principal
O.W. Holmes Middle School/
    Fairfax County Public
    Schools
Alexandria, VA

Sandra Moore, NBCT
High School ELA Teacher
Coupeville High School
Coupeville, WA

Susan E. Schipper
Primary Grade Teacher
Charles Street School
Palmyra, NJ

About the Authors

Paul Bloomberg is a national consultant and the founder and Chief Learning Officer for the Core Collaborative, a professional learning network that specializes in student-centered approaches to learning. Paul is also an Author Consultant for Corwin and a North American consultant for Visible Learning Plus.

Prior to founding The Core Collaborative, he was the former director of TIDES (Transformative Inquiry Design for Effective Schools and Systems), a nonprofit in San Diego focusing on inquiry-based learning. Dr. Bloomberg, a former principal and instructional leader, has directly supported multiple, successful school turn-around and school innovation efforts nationally. He was also a Distinguished Professional Development Associate for the Leadership and Learning Center, founded by Douglas Reeves. He is deeply committed to enhancing student success and believes that we all share in the responsibility for equity and diversity.

Paul's passion is partnering with professional learning teams and systems in an effort to empower ALL students to take ownership of their learning. Paul lives in California with his husband, Tony, and two sons, Alex and Taylor.

Barb Pitchford is a national consultant focusing on leadership for school improvement. During her 30 plus years in public education, Barb has worked at all school levels—high, middle, and elementary—as a teacher, counselor, and administrator. For the past 10 years, Barb has worked as a professional learning consultant specializing in powerful and practical leadership for improved learning for both students *and* teachers. Currently, Barb works with Corwin as a consultant teaching, coaching, and consulting on John Hattie's Visible Learning work, Leading Impact Teams, and is the Executive Director of Professional

Learning and cofounder of The Core Collaborative. Barb's passion is supporting schools to use their greatest resource—their teachers—to build knowledge, skills, and confidence to ensure success for both students and teachers. Based on research around collaboration and formative assessment, Barb specializes in developing Impact Teams to improve teacher expertise and increase student achievement.

Introduction

We began our work together accidently. We both shared a passion for helping and supporting others and we were both relatively new to consulting, having spent our entire careers in schools and districts as part of faculties in some capacity or another, and then both ending up as principals.

As consultants, we occasionally worked with the same schools and districts, and through our work together we soon discovered a shared and deep-seated passion for trying to truly make a difference for kids and a bone deep belief in the extraordinary capacity of teachers. We found ourselves trading ideas, experiences, and new knowledge more and more. We also discovered we shared an unshakeable belief that teachers do serious heavy lifting and need ways to lighten their load while increasing their impact on student learning.

At the same time, John Hattie came up on our radar, and his contributions to what works best in education combined with our knowledge from other education thought leaders and researchers moved us to focusing on two distinct and interrelated high-impact practices: teacher collaboration and the formative assessment process. And the rest is . . . well, not history, it is our book.

This book represents thousands of hours of practice, hundreds of dedicated partner schools and district teams, tons of research, and decades of experience that combine to create what we consider to be a powerful, doable, authentic process that recognizes and builds on teacher expertise and children's innate desire to learn. It is a process that is anchored in creating a learning culture in which teachers and students become confident in their capacity to learn and to succeed—in other words, this process builds a culture of efficacy.

For years we have heard about empowering teachers, about teachers being the number one influence on student learning (they are), about "making" good teachers, etc. We have also heard for years about the importance of teaching kids more than just content (the 3 R's +), but also the "21st Century Skills" such as cooperation, critical thinking, communication, and creativity.

The reality does not often reflect those ideas. Rather, it appears that the residual effect of No Child Left Behind has entrenched the traditional "stand and deliver" model where the teacher delivers the content and the students are receptacles of the information (hope springs eternal). From our experience, this model is alive and well in American classrooms and seems to be the default mode in many classrooms today.

To that end, most teachers in the last decade have been under serious pressure to "raise test scores." In fact, those test scores could very well be tied to the teacher's compensation. These initiatives have promised to get test scores up so districts have "bought" and teachers have "paid" (in time, effort, stress) for one initiative after another, scrambling to learn and try the newest, latest, and greatest silver bullet. It's become an exhausting exercise for most and has rarely yielded positive results.

What has become clear is that the top down all-school or all-district initiatives do not work. It is expensive, exhausting, and in no way empowers teachers or students to be motivated learners. Nor does this model lend itself to teacher and student collaboration, collective inquiry, or innovation. Empowerment is simply not part of this formula.

The reality, in fact, is that teachers and leaders care deeply about kids, work incredibly hard to make a difference, but are often exhausted and frustrated from lack of progress. We get it. We've been there.

So why this book? Our belief and our experience is that every school has what it takes to improve. EVERY school! The resources under the roof of a school building are extraordinary. What is needed is leadership that believes in the capacity of all teachers and all students to learn, to succeed, and to excel. We need leadership that is unafraid to share the responsibility to make authentic learning happen. We need leadership that is willing to commit to creating optimal conditions that build a true learning culture in which everyone is a learner, everyone is learning how to share, to fail, to reflect, to persevere, and to celebrate success.

The last several decades have provided us with extraordinary resources that make it crystal clear what works in schools. We know what it takes to be effective—to be *excellent*. This book is about how to use what schools already have, teacher teams, to operationalize the high-impact practices that empower teachers to make a positive difference for all students. It is real, authentic, doable, and uses the resources every school has: teacher expertise and team time.

Book format: We wrote our book for busy educators. It's straightforward and can be swallowed whole, from beginning to end, or read in chunks, based on your interest and/or need.

Chapter 1 introduces the concept of Impact Teams. It is an overview, somewhat like reading the back cover of a book but with a bit more detail.

Chapters 2 through 7 are all formatted the same way. In fact everything we do uses simple but effective formats. We don't do complicated. Learning is complicated, teaching is complicated, leading is complicated, so why compound already complicated work with complex formats?

Each chapter is organized in the following way:

- A cool quote that pertains to the topic of the chapter
- An appreciative inquiry question that connects your experience to the topic
- The WHAT section succinctly explains the topic being defined
- The WHY section explains why the topic is critical to Impact Team success
- The HOW section describes the process used for implementation
- The NUTSHELL is a summary of the chapter
- The CHECK-IN is a checklist or rubric that gives the perspective Impact Team the opportunity to check where they are at in the Impact Team implementation process. This is essentially a reflection and provides an opportunity to think about where they need/ want to go next.

The Appendices are full of resources that have been created, collected, and adapted for peer facilitators, teachers, leaders, and teams to support Impact Team implementation.

We all learn through experimentation, practice (and more practice), and sharing with one another. We have invited all of our partner districts, schools, teachers, and students to write their own success stories and we are committed to sharing their success! Each story is unique, but all share the same foundation . . . the basics of the Impact Team Model.

Impact Teams create the culture and conditions for every teacher every day to answer the question: "What is my impact?" Impact Teams re-energize teacher teams to believe in their collective capacity to make a difference, to immediately and significantly increase not only student learning but also teacher learning.

Defining Impact Teams

1

"Together, people can accomplish that which one person cannot. Social action depends on the belief that a group can effect change. Collective efficacy helps people realize their shared destiny."

Bandura 1997, 2000

Empowerment: We have partnered with over 300 schools and close to a thousand teams, and we believe that as educators our moral purpose is to create optimal conditions for every learner in the system to develop the belief in their capacity to learn and to ultimately make a difference.

THE WHAT: REFOCUSING PLCS

Kids are struggling to be successful, and so are teachers. Tapping into the structures that already exist in nearly every school in America, team planning time with the Impact Team Model (ITM) refocuses *traditional* professional learning communities (PLCs) by combining two existing practices:

1. The formative assessment process: A *process* that happens in the *classroom* and involves students in every aspect of their own assessment (Stiggins & Chappuis, 2006).

2. Collaborative inquiry: A *process* in which *teacher teams* partner together to understand their impact on student learning and to scale up teacher expertise.

Through efficient and effective collaborative practices, the ITM promotes a school culture in which teachers and students are partners in learning.

Through this partnership, the ITM continuously builds teacher, student, and collective efficacy.

The Classroom

The ITM operationalizes the formative assessment process in the classroom and puts students at the center of the learning. This model requires students to:

- articulate the learning intention and criteria needed for progress and achieve mastery of state standards;
- engage in accurate self- and peer assessment with the goal of being able to explain where they are at in the learning and their next learning steps;
- learn how to give and receive accurate, respectful, descriptive feedback;
- develop challenging and possible (*stretch*) learning goals and revise their work using feedback; and
- monitor their own progress and mastery of state standards.

Teacher Teams

Impact Teams meet frequently to understand their impact on student learning and to take collective action to make a difference for all learners. They meet for the express purpose of learning together in service to all students. ITM creates an efficient structure for teacher teams to engage in collaborative inquiry and use trained peer facilitators to guide their colleagues over time. Leadership makes instructional improvement a priority by actively participating in professional learning.

Impact Teams can take on many forms: grade-level teams, course-alike teams, department or division teams, vertical teams, school-level instructional leadership teams, district leadership teams, and special focus teams (e.g., RTI, child study, etc.).

Eight Purposeful Protocols

In our experience, teams have been asked to do collaborative inquiry but are not given structures to do inquiry effectively. Over the course of the book, you will learn about eight purposeful protocols that teams use to guide collaborative inquiry. These eight protocols are used in every meeting to ensure efficiency and focus and are central to the ITM.

The Difference

The ITM is significantly different from the current practice of most traditional PLCs implemented in schools nationally.

The ITM is NOT:

- A team of teachers solely focused on analyzing benchmark and summative assessment data with little time to respond to student needs
- A method to sort students into ability tracks
- A team whose sole purpose is to fill in a complicated template for accountability purposes
- A team of teachers that meet once a month for compliance and accountability

In reflecting where your team is in the collaborative process and where you want to go with the process, consider the following similarities and differences.

Similarities	Differences
Purpose - Focus on increased student achievement - To improve instructional practices	Purpose - To purposefully strengthen collective teacher efficacy - To empower teachers to improve their practice - To implement the formative assessment process—students being at the center - To create intellectual capital - To build agency - To focus on progress not just achievement - To operationalize the Visible Learning high-impact influences
Protocols - The 4 PLC Questions drive the inquiry - Sharing ideas around effective practice - Norms for effective collaboration	Protocols - Appreciative inquiry: focusing on and learning from what is best in the system - 3-Step (universal) protocol to focus the meeting and to ensure efficiency - Universal protocol is used at all levels of the learning organization - Eight purposeful protocols are used to share and build knowledge aligned to purpose of the meeting (classroom protocols AND team meeting protocols) - Requires student goal setting

(Continued)

(Continued)

Similarities	Differences
• Planning for upcoming instructional units of study	• Requires student self- and peer assessment • Requires weekly meetings • Requires utilization of the formative assessment process • Teachers are not required to grade assessments or exams
Structure • Recursive cycles of collaborative teacher inquiry or action research cycles • Job-alike teams • Shared or distributed leadership	Structure • Variety of team configurations based on purpose • Focus on developing and supporting collective leadership
Evidence of Student Learning • Analysis of data	Evidence of Student Learning • Data is always formative (i.e., student work) • Data is always current, fresh • Assessments are criteria based (rubrics) • Use of multiple-choice items is rare • Student voice data (self- and peer assessment) is used to understand progress of learning

THE WHY: THE POWER OF EFFICACY

Our Educational Landscape

With the enactment of the NCLB legislation (2002), the focus of our schools shifted from an emphasis on learning to one of achievement on standardized tests above all. Superficially this emphasis did not appear to be very different from previous eras of "school reform"; however, the last decade has clearly shown us that achievement and learning are not synonymous. Simply put, achievement is the arm of accountability, while learning is the life skill. With accountability being the unyielding force, learning is often compromised. Unfortunately the victims of the drive to raise test scores are both the students and the teachers.

An unrelenting focus on absolute achievement has had a significant impact on the culture of many of our schools and has directly and negatively impacted teachers' sense of efficacy, collectively and individually (Finnigan & Daly, 2013). Admittedly the stakes are high for our teachers, leaders, and schools so the drive for achievement regarding high stakes testing is understandable. However, along the way we often sacrificed the notion of learning in our quest for "[a]ll students will be proficient or above."

Thankfully, the winds are shifting with the passing of the ESSA legislation (December, 2015) to a more balanced approach to accountability. However, changing the decade plus practices of accountability by annual test results will take time. We designed the ITM for schools to use as a tool to move from the practice of summative tests to drive instruction to the practice of using the formative assessment process to monitor and support student growth and to instructionally respond to diverse learning needs.

Beware another initiative? Or a way to repurpose existing practices to have greater impact? We are practitioners working in all sizes, sorts, and flavors of schools. We are currently partnering in over 138 schools across the nation from rural to urban to suburban. We know from experience that in our current educational landscape, when educators hear the words *reform* or *assessment*, they think *test* or *check-lists*. When they think *test*, they think or say the following:

- I will be judged or evaluated by this.
- It takes away from my teaching time.
- It takes too much time to grade.
- The at-risk children never do well on tests.
- It shuts down kids who are struggling.

The ITM is a strengths-based model in which the focus is to help teacher teams discover what works well in their school and build upon their existing strengths. Our intention is not to fix broken students, teachers, or systems. Our intention is to support schools by creating conditions where innovation and creativity thrive. "When people focus on human ideals and achievements, peak experiences, and best practices, these things—not the conflicts—tend to flourish" (Mohr & Watkins, 2002).

We must never forget that our core business *is* learning, not dispensing information, not raising test scores, not clever pedagogy, not technology tools. And the learning is not just about student learning. Our role and responsibility is to relentlessly learn together to ensure student progress. Learning together at its best results in a pervasive attitude of "We can do this!" School cultures grounded in the commitment to and practice of learning together are schools in which efficacy thrives. Restoring the belief that teachers as a group can and do make a difference is the impetus of our Impact Team Model.

The Research

In Hattie's (2009) seminal meta-analytic synthesis, *Visible Learning*, he identified the effect of 138 influences on achievement using effect size calculations. Considering that a .40 effect size (ES) is about 1 year's growth in 1 year's time, it is incumbent upon education leaders and teachers to pay attention to those influences that ensure at least a year's progress in a year's time for *all* students.

The development and design of the ITM is based on extensive research that identifies those practices that maximize student learning. Impact Teams operationalize multiple influences that are proven to have the highest effect on student learning. The following are a sample of several high-impact influences used in the ITM:

- Teacher-Student Relationships: .72 ES
- Feedback: .75 ES
- Teacher Clarity: .75 ES
- Formative Evaluation: .90 ES
- Microteaching: .88 ES
- Success Criteria: 1.13 ES
- Assessment Capable Learners: 1.44 ES
- Collective Teacher Efficacy: 1.57 ES

The Power of Efficacy

Bandura (1994, 1997) recognized that academic progress in a school is not only a reflection of the sum of the individual contributions, but also comes from the collective whole, the ways in which the teachers work together. Bandura found that a collective sense of efficacy among a school community contributes significantly to academic achievement. In fact, it was a more powerful predictor than socioeconomic status and as powerful as prior academic achievement.

THE HOW: THE STEPS TO SUCCESS

The design of this book is intended for instructional leadership teams, instructional leaders, or teacher teams who want to expand their collaborative practices regarding the formative assessment process. Each chapter clearly defines the success criteria for successful implementation of this model with chapter Check-Ins.

The Steps to Success

- Chapter 2: Building a Culture of Efficacy
  - What: Defining collective efficacy
  - Why: Impact on student learning
  - How: Strategic planning for strengthening collective efficacy
  - Check-In: System assessment

- Chapter 3: Teaming to Learn
  - What: Effective learning teams
  - Why: Building collective efficacy
  - How: Network, process, and structure
  - Check-In: Team assessment

- Chapter 4: Strengthening Student Efficacy: The Formative Assessment Process in Action
  - What: Partnering with students in the assessment process
  - Why: Building student efficacy
  - How: Three protocols to expand quality formative assessment (EAA Classroom, Microteaching, Lesson Study)
  - Check-In: The formative assessment process

- Chapter 5: Creating Context for Efficacy
  - What: Equitable, viable, and coherent curriculum
  - Why: Teacher and student clarity, strengthening efficacy
  - How: Two protocols for curriculum clarity (Unpacking for Success & Calibration)
  - Check-In: Curriculum checklist

- Chapter 6: Evidence to Inform and Act
  - What: Quality evidence
  - Why: Springboard for action
  - How: Three protocols to inform and act (EAA Team Meeting, Check-In and Case Study, Evidence Walks)
  - Check-In: Analyzing student work

- Chapter 7: Leading Model Teams
  - What: Leading effective learning teams
  - Why: Creating capacity from within to strengthen collective efficacy
  - How: Gradual release
  - Check-In

- Appendices

Building a Culture of Efficacy

2

"As teachers in a school feel empowered to do great things, great things happen."

Eells, 2011

Mastery Moment: Think of a situation in which you felt such confidence and optimism that you believed anything was possible. Why was that belief so strong? What were the conditions that created those powerful feelings?

THE WHAT: THE FOUR SOURCES OF EFFICACY

Efficacy is a word that is often misunderstood. It seems and feels like it should have something to do with effectiveness and efficiency. And it does, sort of. *Efficacy* is defined as the ability to produce a desired or intended effect. It is about the *belief* in the ability to effect change. Imagine a school where efficacy is pervasive, where teachers and students alike believe in their capacity to learn no matter what the challenge, a school where growth mindset prevails—a culture of efficacy.

Taken a step further, collective efficacy is more than collaboration, more than a team of teachers getting together to talk to each other every Wednesday afternoon. Collective efficacy is the result of collaborating *effectively* over time, through thick and thin, collaboration that results in the group's collective *belief* in their power to effect positive change. It is knowledge building through learning from one another. It is the optimism, confidence, and resiliency that evolve from successful learning experiences for both teachers and students.

Impact Teams are a vehicle to develop and nurture efficacy. An *Impact Team* is a network of educators who partner with students and each other in learning. It is a team that is committed to understanding their impact on learning. The stronger the beliefs they hold about their collective capabilities, the more they achieve. Impact Teams empower learners to own and take charge of their learning. Ultimately, they build a culture of efficacy.

Understanding Self-Efficacy

To understand collective teacher efficacy, one must understand self-efficacy. As stated previously, self-efficacy reflects one's confidence in his or her ability to achieve a goal or outcome (Bandura, 1997). It is what we all strive for both personally and professionally. The human drive to be efficacious has resulted in a multi-billion-dollar industry around self-actualization, health and fitness, business, and all sorts of purported pathways to personal success.

Ultimately, however, self-efficacy is a belief in one's ability to succeed. Not surprisingly, self-efficacy has a significant relationship to success and is highly correlated to confidence and optimism.

Four Sources of Self-Efficacy

Efficacy sounds and feels like something we all want in spades and a quality we want to develop in all our students. So our guiding question in our deep dive into the research around efficacy was "What does it take to develop efficacy?"

There are four major sources that contribute to the development of self-efficacy beliefs (Bandura, 1977; Hoy, 2000)

- Mastery Experiences: Having successful experiences influences your perspective of your abilities. These experiences boost self-efficacy. This is the most robust source of efficacy.
- Vicarious Experiences: We define this as having *models of success*. Models of success are an integral source of self-efficacy. Observing someone else perform a task or handle a situation effectively can help you to perform the same task by imitation.
- Social and Verbal Persuasion: We loosely define this as *feedback*. Self-efficacy can be boosted when credible communication and descriptive feedback is given in an effort to guide and motivate learners to successfully complete a task.
- Positive Emotional State: We interpret this as *safety*. A learner must feel safe. The feeling of safety creates a positive emotional state and a willingness to take risks, and make and embrace mistakes as learning opportunities. The feeling of safety can boost self-efficacy.

Student Self-Efficacy

In the much-researched area of efficacy and motivation, student self-efficacy takes center stage. In the context of schools, self-efficacy is a belief in one's capabilities to learn and achieve the intended learning intention. In the classroom setting, student self-efficacy can be seen as a strong "I can" attitude. In contrast, a student with a low sense of self-efficacy tends to believe "I can't" when given a learning task. Often the negative perception is specific to the academic content, such as, "I'm not a good writer" or "I'm not good at Math."

Students who have a strong sense of self-efficacy:

- Are intrinsically motivated and put forth a high degree of effort
- Challenge themselves with difficult tasks
- Are persistent—show grit
- Are resilient and see mistakes as learning opportunities
- Are confident about achieving personal goals

Students are not born with self-efficacy; rather it is acquired in the same way adults build self-efficacy, that is, through:

- Mastery moments
- Models of success
- Feedback
- Safety

The good news is that these four sources of self-efficacy are inherent in the formative assessment process and are an integral component of the Impact Team Model. Specific teaching strategies such as cooperative learning, student goal setting, revision, self- and peer assessment also strengthen student self-efficacy (Fencl & Scheel, 2005). In a student-centered classroom where self-regulation is taught, modeled, and expected, developing self-efficacy is built into the learning process.

Teacher Self-Efficacy

Teacher self-efficacy is defined as the teacher's confidence in his or her ability to promote student learning (Hoy, 2000). This was first discussed as a concept more than 35 years ago. Teachers' self-efficacy is specific to their perception about their own capabilities to foster students' learning and engagement. It is a belief about one's ability to promote positive change for students and has proven to have a positive influence not only on student achievement but also on motivation (Moolenaar, Sleegers & Daly, 2011) and positive attitudes toward school (Miskel, McDonald,

& Bloom, 1983). This confidence and optimism lead to perseverance and commitment to reach and often exceed learning goals.

A teacher's level of confidence about his or her ability to promote learning can depend on past experiences and on the school culture. In his review of the research, Jerald (2007) highlights some teacher behaviors that are found to be related to a teacher's sense of efficacy.

Teachers with a strong sense of efficacy:

- Tend to exhibit greater levels of planning and organization
- Are more open to new ideas and are more willing to experiment with new methods to better meet the needs of their students
- Are more persistent and resilient when things do not go smoothly
- Are less critical of students when they make mistakes
- Are less inclined to refer a difficult student to special education

In an interview with Anita Woolfolk, a researcher in the field of teacher efficacy, Shaughnessy (2004) describes practical implications of the teacher efficacy research:

Teachers who set goals, who persist, who try another strategy when one approach is found wanting—in other words, teachers who have a high sense of efficacy and act on it—are more likely to have students who learn. (pp. 156–157)

Collective Teacher Efficacy

Rooted in self-efficacy, *collective efficacy* is defined as a group's shared beliefs about their collective capability to promote successful student outcomes within their school (Goddard, Hoy, Hoy, 2000). Collective efficacy involves more than positive thinking. It is ultimately tied to collective action, the ability to make things happen. This ability is defined as *agency.*

Building a culture of efficacy requires system-wide focus on strengthening student and teacher self-efficacy. Eells (2011) states that collective teacher efficacy is the pervasive belief that directly affects the school's ability to increase achievement. At the heart of the Impact Team Model is the belief that the learners in the system can make a difference and impact learning for ALL.

THE WHY: RESEARCH AND REASONS

Strengthening efficacy at all levels of the school dramatically improves student learning. If teachers and students feel powerful they can surmount obstacles and persist when challenged and expend the necessary effort to learn. We have highlighted the following four reasons:

Reason 1: Has the Greatest Influence on Student Learning

John Hattie (2014) identified *collective teacher efficacy* (CTE) as the single most powerful influence on student achievement. With an effect size* of 1.57, collective teacher efficacy can quadruple the rate of student learning (Eells, 2011). In fact, in a study by Hoy, Sweetland, and Smith (2002), they found that collective teacher efficacy had a greater influence on student achievement than socioeconomic status.

*Effect size: .40 is about 1 year's growth in 1 year's time.

Reason 2: Creates and Sustains a Learning Culture

When emphasis is placed on intentionally planning for the four sources of efficacy, building knowledge together around effective practice is the result. Knowledge building and knowledge sharing thrive in a learning culture. Teachers and students not only learn at an accelerated rate, but they also learn how to learn, how to self-regulate, how to persevere, how to communicate, and how to problem solve.

Reason 3: Focuses on System Strength

When the mission of the school is to ensure mastery experiences, it focuses the system on building off of people's strengths instead of identifying deficits. The studies on positive imagery suggest that employees who hold self-images of competence and success are more likely to achieve high levels of performance than those with poor self-esteem (Mohr & Watkins, 2002).

Reason 4: Creates a Healthy Climate

Learning is accelerated when people feel safe. Having a faculty that believes that it can accomplish great things is vital for the health of a school (Eells, 2011). Imagine coming to a school where making mistakes is understood as part of the learning process. Imagine coming to a school where students and teachers embrace the notion of taking risks and seek opportunities to learn more.

THE HOW: PLANNING FOR EFFICACY

You have the power to build a culture of efficacy! But you have to plan for it. Fundamental to developing self- and collective efficacy are the four sources of efficacy.

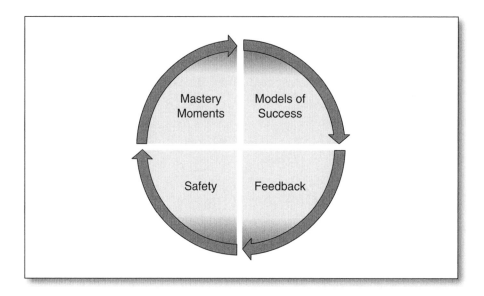

To build a culture of efficacy school-wide, leadership teams need to intentionally and thoughtfully develop a plan that provides for multiple and ongoing opportunities for teacher teams to experience the four sources of efficacy.

1. **Mastery Moments**: To build confidence, teams need to experience success. Teacher teams need direct experience that they interpret as successful. These successes increase confidence and build resiliency. Interestingly, the research makes it clear that easy success does not contribute to building a sense of collective efficacy. In fact, quick and easy success followed by failure will produce discouragement (Goddard et al., 2000). However, teams who take on challenging goals and overcome obstacles to realize success come away with a robust belief in their collective efficacy.

2. **Models of Success:** Learning from others' successes is another way to build efficacy. Experiences in which teams of teachers observe the successful practices of other teams and/or schools provide indirect experiences that translate into doable practice. Think of this source as modeling effective practice. Teams observe successful teams and then see themselves as capable of performing similarly.

3. **Feedback**: We know that feedback doubles the rate of learning, and that's not just for students. We learn through descriptive timely feedback. Teams who collectively focus on getting better, commit to doing the research, taking the risks, and sharing knowledge and skills, use feedback as a tool for learning from one another. But not all feedback is created

equal and not all feedback is heard. A key ingredient to effective teams is diving deeply into productive feedback practices. Feedback moves the group forward in ways that are positive, appreciative, and productive. With forward movement, success is possible, and with success, comes the possibility of increasing collective efficacy.

4. **Safety**: Relational trust is key to building effective teams and an essential ingredient in building collective efficacy. Relational trust in teams translates into team members who genuinely listen to one another, who respect others' opinions even if they differ from their own, who willingly share knowledge, and who feel accepted, respected, and empowered by their teammates. To build trust, first teams need to take their "trust temperature." There are several trust surveys available online (e.g., Tschannen-Moran, Hoy, & Hoy). With baseline data of the level of trust, teams then commit to collaborate on ways to build trust where it might be weak. Checking the trust temp every 3 to 4 months is good practice and ensures the continued commitment to a safe team environment.

Team Reflection: *List some ways your leadership team provides opportunities for teams to:*

- Experience mastery moments;
- Share successful models;
- Learn to effectively give and receive descriptive feedback; and
- Create a safe team environment for learning.

NUTSHELL

What we have identified in the preceding pages are the roots of efficacy at the student, teacher, and collective levels. And while student and teacher efficacy is correlated to improved achievement, collective teacher efficacy accelerates learning at an even greater rate. Quite simply, sharing knowledge and developing skills together reaps significant gains. Goddard, Hoy, and Hoy (2000) suggest that to improve student achievement systemwide it is crucial to raise the collective efficacy beliefs of the staff. Believing in the combined intellect, shared commitment, and focused energy of the group moves a school to even greater learning and higher impact.

When teachers believe that they can get through to all students, even the most difficult ones who may be hard to reach, they have collective efficacy. The Impact Team Model is explicitly designed to build teacher, student, and collective efficacy. This pervasive belief directly affects the school's ability to increase achievement (Eells, 2011).

CHECK-IN

Where is your team on the collective teacher efficacy (CTE) continuum?

Collective Teacher Efficacy Continuum	
High CTE	**Low CTE**
Optimistic: Have a shared belief that all students can achieve at least 1 year's growth in 1 year's time (growth mindset).	**Pervasive doubt:** Feel powerless over circumstances beyond their control, expect undesirable results (deficit mindset).
Confidence: Believe they can effectively teach students so that every student makes a year's growth in a year's time.	**Uncertainty**: Doubt that they can teach or touch certain students.
Collaborative: Believe in the power of collective thought and action.	**Isolated**: Believe that they are alone in their specific responsibilities and challenges, doubt that the team/group can add value.
Learners all: See themselves as learners, value error, seek feedback, learn from one another.	**Know enough**: See themselves as experts and know enough to deliver what needs to be taught.
Perseverance: Staying power based on commitment to success.	**Apathy:** Feel powerless, put in minimum effort.

←——————————————————————————————————————→

High CTE   Low CTE

Activity

Planning for CTE must be purposeful. With your instructional leadership team, use this organizer to develop a plan for strengthening CTE.

Fold a piece of chart paper into fourths. Label each box accordingly. With a green marker list the ways you are purposefully planning for each one of the four sources of efficacy. With a blue marker, write down ideas you have in each box that would help your team be more purposeful in strengthening CTE at your school.

Mastery Moments	Model of Success
Example: Teachers video record examples of effective practice.	*Example: Teachers watch effective teaching videos and discuss what made the practice effective.*
Feedback	Safety
Example: Noting strengths, the principal gives positive feedback as she does evidence walks regarding practices specific to the school focus.	*Example: The staff takes a relational trust survey and discusses the results and action steps three times during the year.*

Teaming to Learn 3

"Good schools depend heavily on cooperative endeavors. Relational trust is the connective tissue that binds individuals together to advance the education and welfare of students. Improving schools requires us to think harder about how best to organize the work of adults and students so that this connective tissue remains healthy and strong."

Bryk & Schneider, 2003

Mastery Moment: Think of a time that you were part of an effective team. What conditions were in place for that team to be effective?

THE WHAT: TEAMING TO LEARN

Professional collaboration is the activity of learning together to generate new ideas, solve problems, and collectively improve practice. And by collectively improving practice, teams begin to see positive changes in learning. These mastery moments strengthen collective efficacy.

Teachers in the system have varying levels of self-efficacy regarding their craft. When teachers collaborate with other teachers who have high levels of self-efficacy they tend to develop higher efficacy beliefs as well (Siciliano, 2016). Therefore, collaboration is essential in building a culture of efficacy.

However, learning together is easier said than done. Here's the reality. Almost 90% of teachers are part of a team. Most teachers spend less than 1 hour per week formally (scheduled time) collaborating with colleagues. Given the 40 hours a week we work in school (not counting the many hours *outside* of school we prepare, worry, plan, etc.), that's about 2.5%.

So what can teams do to make the time spent with colleagues so valuable that they *can't wait* to get to their team meeting to share, to learn, to debate, to celebrate? What can teams do to make their time together not just productive, but a powerful tool to improve teaching that actually has an impact on student learning? After all, isn't that why we collaborate?

Google recently conducted a 3-year study on teaming called Project Aristotle (Graham, 2016). Not surprisingly, they found that working effectively together can reap powerful results: that deep and innovative thinking come from interactive problem solving. Most businesses now work in teams. Isolation and autonomy are OUT; teaming and collaboration are IN! Simply put, *we* is smarter than *me*.

Working with schools across the nation and at all levels, learning from missteps and mistakes, we have developed a collaborative model that operationalizes what we know makes teams highly effective and remarkably efficient, and that continuously builds collective efficacy. This model, called the Impact Team Model (ITM), refocuses traditional professional learning communities (PLCs) and teacher teams on two specific areas:

1. the critical partnership between teachers and students in the deep implementation of the formative assessment process

2. on learning how to authentically and deeply learn together to scale up teacher expertise using action research cycles

Effective Learning Teams

We know exactly what makes teacher teams productive (and what does not). Gallimore, Emerling, Saunders, and Goldenberg (2009) cite five components:

1. Job-alike teams (common relevant focus)

2. Clear goals

3. Trained peer facilitator

4. Inquiry-based protocols

5. Stable settings (protected time, principal commits to the process over time)

Recently, a paper out of Harvard Graduate School of Education by Johnson, Reinhorn, and Simon (Shafer, 2016) examines how collaboration works best, listing five factors that contribute to a team's success:

1. Clear worthwhile purpose

2. Sufficient regular time

3. Administrative support and attention

4. Trained teacher facilitators

5. Integrated approach to teacher support

We have identified seven components of effective learning teams and operationalized them through the ITM:

1. A commitment to high expectations and strengthening learner efficacy

2. The principal promoting and participating in team learning and team development

3. Meeting weekly to be responsive to student and teacher needs

4. Recursive inquiry cycles (action research) based on the eight Impact Teams Purposeful Protocols (see p. 30)

5. Trained peer facilitation

6. A commitment to strengthening relational trust

7. Making use of purposeful, descriptive feedback

THE WHY: RESEARCH AND REASONS

Developing collective capacity through effective teaming is how schools get better. Michael Fullan (2010) confirms this assertion: "Collective capacity generates emotional commitment and the technical expertise that no amount of individual capacity working alone can come close to matching." Teachers can no longer work in isolation. To meet the current and diverse demands of their students, they must learn to learn together. Although there are many reasons why it is important to team, we have highlighted the following four reasons:

Reason 1: Strengthens the Culture of Learning

The ITM creates conditions for a learning culture to exist. Gruenert and Whitaker (2015) describe six types of learning cultures:

1. Collaborative—embraces learning for all students and adults, feedback flourishes

2. Comfortable-Collaborative—polite to the point of inhibiting constructive feedback

3. Contrived-Collegial—leadership determines how the faculty behaves

4. Balkanized—encourages small group competition

5. Fragmented—everyone does their own thing

6. Toxic—negativism is pervasive

In the hundreds of schools we have worked with, we have found that most schools see themselves as collaborative. However, when taking a closer look at their operating systems and the beliefs behind those, most are more of a "contrived collegial" culture where teachers are scheduled to meet in teams to do the work assigned. Grade-level or course-alike meetings become a "TO DO LIST" of action items, including looking at data to fill in a template for site and district leadership. Accountability rather than learning is the driving force.

In contrast, the ITM focuses on critical components of a learning culture:

- Create ways to share and develop knowledge
- Build on the strengths of the teachers and students
- Learn from models of success
- Create opportunities to experience mastery moments

Reason 2: Teacher Quality Improves

Teachers get better together. Teachers and schools that engage in better quality collaboration have greater achievement gains in math and reading (Ronfeldt, Farmer, McQueen, & Grissom, 2015). Vanderbilt Associate Professor Jason Grissom said, "Focusing on building teacher teams and providing meaningful ways for teachers to work together on the tough challenges they encounter can lead to substantively important achievement gains" (Ronfeldt et al., 2015). In fact, teacher quality improves at greater rates when they work in schools where collaboration is of better quality (Ronfeldt et al., 2015).

Reason 3: Relationships Matter

Leana (2011) of the University of Pittsburgh talks about teacher collaboration in terms of human capital and social capital. Human capital is specific to developing the individual teacher—that is, subject area expertise, pedagogical skills, and so on—whereas social capital focuses on developing relationships among teachers. It's not just about what the teacher knows, but where and how he or she gets that knowledge. Leana's study showed that social capital had a multiplier effect on human capital. There are strong student achievement gains when teachers have frequent conversations with colleagues centered on teaching and learning and when there is a feeling of trust or closeness among teachers (Bryk & Schneider, 2003).

Reason 4: Increased Student Achievement

In a 5-year study of Title 1 schools serving more than 14,000 students, Gallimore, Emerling, and their team (2009) found that teacher learning teams contributed significantly to overall school improvement. They found that after schools converted routine meetings to teacher learning teams focusing on student learning, achievement rose by 41% overall and by 54% for Hispanic students.

Schools cannot improve without a way to constantly learn. Collaborative inquiry and action research are the vehicles for ongoing, job embedded, professional learning. Impact Teams are strategically designed to build teacher expertise through dynamic and deep collaborative learning.

THE HOW: ARCHITECTURE OF THE IMPACT TEAM MODEL

High performance teams need architecture; they need a design to be productive. Impact Teams have a specific infrastructure to do the work. The bricks and mortar are the organizational structures and processes required to do business. The infrastructure of the ITM includes:

- The learning network
- The process
- The structure

In the following pages we unpack each component. The diagram on page 28 provides a visual representation of the Impact Team infrastructure.

THE LEARNING NETWORK

Effective collaboration is dependent on the quality of the learning network. We have identified three foundational components:

1. Purpose

2. Trust

3. Communication

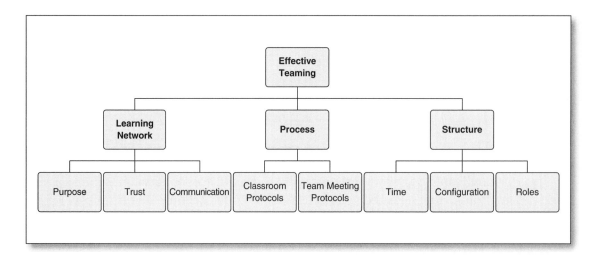

Purpose

The first order of the collaborative process is to devote time to identifying and solidifying the **purpose** of the "teaming" and the underlying beliefs of the team members. A team is a group of people with a common purpose. The ultimate purpose of Impact Teams is to strengthen efficacy: (1) teacher efficacy, (2) student efficacy, and (3) collective teacher efficacy. With purpose comes commitment, and the commitment builds the synergy that moves the team forward.

Following purpose, the team needs to identify their **shared beliefs** underpinning the purpose. Beliefs are powerful predictors of behavior. Carol Dweck (2006) identifies two types of beliefs or, in her words, *mindsets—* growth and fixed. John Hattie (2012) calls these beliefs *mindframes.* He describes mind frames as "ways of thinking" that drive our practices. Several of the Hattie mind frames have particular relevance to deep implementation of Impact Teams:

- We see ourselves as evaluators of the effect of our teaching on student learning
- We talk more about the learning than the teaching
- We are change agents
- We see assessment as feedback
- We are collaborators

Impact Teams think deeply together about the beliefs that ground their thinking, their decisions, and their actions around teaching and learning. From that deep foundation, shared understanding and trust begin to develop.

Trust

Relational trust is the connective tissue of working relationships and is central to building effective learning communities. Do not underestimate the importance of trust in the learning process. Learning can be risky business, exposing our lack of knowledge and learning through mistakes and failures. Relational trust is grounded in social respect; without respect, collaborative learning ceases. Building trust within the school community is essential. In general, trust building is a slow process, but it can be accelerated with peer facilitation and modeling of transparency and risk-taking, open interaction, and effective and transparent communication systems.

Being intentional about measuring and monitoring team trust is an important practice in the ITM. There are a variety of tools available that can be used as an entry point to opening dialogue on team trust (see Appendices).

Team Trust: *Have your team take the team trust survey in Appendix G. Discuss the results with your team. Make a plan to periodically check your team's level of trust.*

Communication

Without effective communication systems in place and used relentlessly, none of the above will result in ongoing collaborative learning. The following are key to a robust and vibrant communication system:

- Establishing systems of communication for all stakeholders that are agreed on, systemized, and transparent
- Cloud services—shared folders, Google Docs, or other platforms that are accessible and transparent for meeting notes, student work samples, standards, curriculum, and assessment works-in-progress
- Meeting notes: Use a simple but complete template that captures the critical information from the meetings and is then uploaded to the cloud service for all to access (see Appendix D)

Keep in mind that developing collective expertise is the heart of the ITM and without a bullet-proof system of communication, building knowledge and skills will be inconsistent and diluted.

Team Reflection

- *If you asked members of your team what the **purpose** of their team is, would their answers be similar? If yes, why? If no, why not?*

- *What is your team's understanding of collective teacher efficacy and the impact it has on student learning?*

THE PROCESS: EIGHT PURPOSEFUL PROTOCOLS

The ITM uses eight purposeful protocols to guide collaborative inquiry. We have categorized the protocols into the context in which they are used.

Team Protocols: Teams need rules of engagement and structures to make team meetings efficient and effective. Team meeting protocols were born out of what effective teams need to learn about:

- getting to know standards and/or creating rubric-bound assessments
- calibrating student work samples
- sharing and trying out innovative teaching strategies
- engaging in lesson study
- applying the formative assessment process in the classroom
- analyzing impact through the analysis of student work

Classroom Protocols: Routines and processes are the backbone of daily classroom life. Efficient routines make it easier for students and teachers to learn and achieve. Classroom protocols have been developed to guide students in:

- understanding the learning intention
- understanding the criteria for success
- giving and receiving evidence-based feedback
- effective self- and peer assessment
- reflective goal setting

The ITM eight purposeful protocols have been adapted from common protocols that we have encountered in our work with teams. The ITM protocols have been field tested nationally to ensure efficiency and practicality, keeping in mind that learning teams have limited time for collaborative inquiry. We have also infused the use of video into many of our protocols, since video is an efficient, powerful medium to enhance teaching and learning. In addition, all the ITM protocols are anchored in the process, Evidence • Analysis • Action (EAA). Teams use quality EVIDENCE to ANALYZE what impact their ACTIONS have on the learner. EAA sets the team up for inquiry and action research. Quite simply, EAA is how we do business.

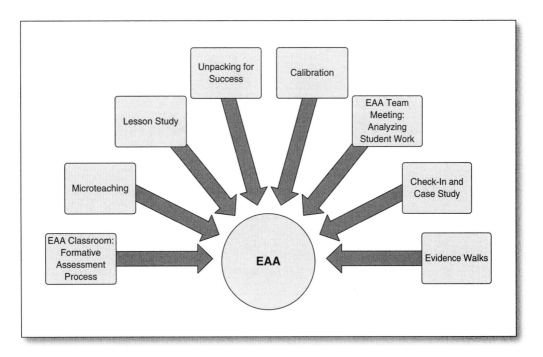

The protocols are separated into three categories (see below): (1) classroom protocols, (2) team meeting protocols, and (3) combination of both. Each protocol is used purposefully to guide collaborative inquiry.

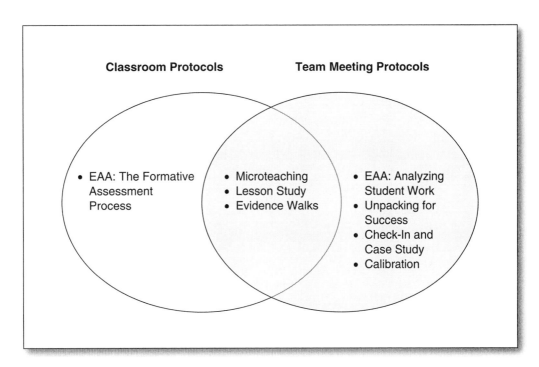

The Classroom Protocol

When routines and procedures are carefully taught, modeled, and established in the classroom, students know what is expected of them and learn how to function as independent learners. Having these predictable patterns in place allows teachers to spend more time leveraging evidence-based feedback. The EAA protocol is used to expand the formative assessment process into classroom culture. This protocol is described fully in Chapter 4.

Evidence • Analysis • Action: Classroom

This protocol is the heart of the ITM since it operationalizes the formative assessment process in regular classroom instruction. When teachers and students use the three-step EAA protocol, they learn how to apply success criteria, how to self- and peer assess, how to give and receive feedback, and finally how to set goals and determine next steps in the learning process. Partnering with students in this process is a critical component of the formative assessment process (O'Connell & Vandas, 2015).

Our ultimate goal is for students to be able to independently assess their own learning. This helps them gauge where they need extra help and where they are doing well enough to move on. Hattie (2009) refers to this process as developing assessment capable learners; this practice more than triples the rate of learning (1.44 effect size). The EAA classroom protocol is unique to the ITM; in our experience we have found no other PLC frameworks that put students at the center.

Team Meeting Protocols

In addition to guiding the team's inquiry, protocols create recurring opportunities for teachers to contribute their knowledge, creativity, and skills. We use protocols purposefully to focus meetings and to ensure efficiency, to avoid wasting time, and to stimulate depth of thinking and quality dialogue. Protocols help

- increase equity (no one person overwhelms the conversation);
- establish transparency (all voices heard);
- promote participation (all voices welcome);
- distribute leadership (multiple and situational leaders); and
- focus the conversation (stick to the learning goal).

Based on the research and our experience, we have learned that effective teams participate in the following collective actions to improve student learning. Effective team protocols consist of steps familiar to educators including

- jointly identifying goals for student learning,
- finding or developing assessments of student progress toward those goals,
- adopting research-based approaches to address the goals,
- planning and delivering lessons everyone tries,
- using classroom performance data to evaluate the commonly planned and delivered lessons, and
- reflecting on student gains to determine next steps.

The following protocols are used by Impact Teams during collaborative inquiry cycles.

- ***Evidence • Analysis • Action (EAA: Analyzing Student Work):*** Impact Teams use this three-step protocol to analyze student work efficiently to take collective action. The focus is to understand their impact on learning. They collaborate to share their expertise, thereby strengthening collective teacher efficacy. There are many protocols used nationally to analyze student work; however, teams can use our EAA team meeting protocol successfully in about 45 to 50 minutes. Teams will walk away with a detailed, clear, and practical plan grounded in strategies that get the highest effect regarding advancing student learning. An example of how this protocol is used is described in Chapters 6 and 7.
- ***Check-In/Case Study:*** Monitoring instructional effectiveness based on student progress is often a well-intentioned agreement but forgotten in the reality of the busyness of school life. The purpose of this protocol is to ensure that teams monitor the implementation and effectiveness of the team's collective actions. During the learning cycle, the team frequently checks in with each other to share successes and challenges and make necessary course corrections. In this protocol, each teacher chooses a student who is representative of a learning group and/or demographic group (e.g., an ELL student or an at-risk student or gifted and talented student, etc.). They use these students' work samples to make generalizations about teaching effectiveness by learning group. An example for how this protocol is used is in Chapter 6.
- ***Unpacking for Success:*** This protocol is designed for teams to get to know the standards. It ensures that the team is on the same page regarding learning outcomes as well as aligned in their approach to teaching the standard(s). Using this protocol gives teams the necessary understanding to partner with students in the formative assessment process. It engages teams in the following:

- ○ Researching the standard,
- ○ Defining the key concepts and skills,
- ○ Defining cognitive rigor for task development,
- ○ Agreeing on relevance and big ideas and/or essential understandings,
- ○ Determining key competencies, and
- ○ Developing rubric-bound formative assessments.

This protocol is different than other unpacking or unwrapping protocols since it puts emphasis on understanding learning progressions, relevant student products and/or performances, and support for developing learning intentions and success criteria for daily instruction. An example for how this protocol is used in context is located in Chapter 5.

- • **Calibration:** This protocol is designed to ensure that all members of the team are accurately scoring student work and that they are consistent in their scoring. In the formative assessment process, student work is evaluated based on the success criteria developed in the Unpacking for Success protocol. Using student work samples from different levels, teachers anchor their understanding of progress through the calibration process. A description of this protocol can be found in Chapter 6.

Combination Protocols

We have found that some protocols can be used in both contexts: (1) the classroom, and (2) the team meeting. These three protocols have been adapted for the ITM to enhance the team's implementation of the formative assessment process. As described earlier in this chapter, they are also grounded in the three-step process: Evidence • Analysis • Action.

Evidence Walks

Evidence walks are a form of instructional rounds (much like medical rounds) that help teachers and leaders look closely at a specific and predetermined practice central to the formative assessment process. Seeing the practice in real time (evidence) and providing feedback and support to improve practice is the essence of evidence walks. In small groups, teachers and leaders observe a colleague's classroom (volunteer) looking for evidence related to the practice. After the observation, the team provides *nonjudgmental* descriptive feedback (analysis) based on predetermined specific criteria for that practice. Based on the feedback, the team identifies next steps (action). A full description of this protocol in action can be found in Chapter 6.

Microteaching

Microteaching is organized practice teaching that provides Impact Team members the opportunity to try out small parts of lessons and/or strategies specific to the formative assessment with one another, without students present. This reduces the variable of the students so teams get to practice new strategies *before* they try them in the classroom. The team can also view video from an open source provider like The Teaching Channel or Teacher Tube. The team observes the video and provides positive, specific feedback. Then, each member of the team has an opportunity to try the technique observed. This practice can be done in small teams, or teachers can practice the strategy in front of the team. The team then summarizes what was learned after the session is complete.

Lesson Study

Like microteaching, Impact Teams use lesson study to improve instructional effectiveness specific to the formative assessment process. It is a collaborative learning process in which teacher teams examine their practice from the planning stage through teaching, observing, and critiquing. The team creates a detailed lesson plan that one teacher teaches and the others observe. The focus of the observation is on the students' responses rather than the teacher's actions. Based on the evidence, the team revises the lesson.

Team Reflection: *What protocols does your team currently use? How do they support team learning?*

Purposeful Protocol Icon: This icon will be used to indicate application of the protocols by the team.

Additional Resources: The templates for each protocol can be found in Appendix A. In addition, there are two examples of Impact Teams inquiry cycles in Appendix E.

THE STRUCTURE

The nuts and bolts of collaboration are what it takes to operationalize the model. If they are not in place, collaboration will be haphazard and catch as catch can. If the team meeting is not structured, then there's a good chance the meeting won't result in authentic collaboration.

Time

Impact Teams need sufficient and protected time to meet to be effective. If time is not protected and interruptions are allowed, the ITM will not have the opportunity to do the work.

- Impact Teams meet weekly (45–60 minutes). This is *protected* time and never superseded by other busyness. Principals whose schools are consistently high performing dedicate and protect time for teacher collaboration.
- Instructional Leadership Teams meet monthly (60–90 minutes) to guide, support, and monitor school-wide Impact Teams.

Team Configuration

Teams are configured multiple ways based on their purpose and the common goal of the team. For example:

- Elementary: grade-level teams
- Secondary: course-alike teams
- Curricular: vertical teams
- Intervention (RTI, child study teams, etc.): representation from key teaching areas and support services
- Instructional Leadership team: lead teachers and/or peer facilitators from all Impact Teams

Regardless of the makeup of the team, the key is to bring people together to generate ideas, solve problems, and learn from one another firmly anchored in a common purpose, that is, to empower learners.

Roles

Team roles are identified and followed with the team conjointly determining what roles are necessary and the job description of each. We define *roles* as useful behaviors that contribute to the team's effectiveness. Each member of the team adopts a role. The key is for the roles to be clear, for the members to have (or develop) the skills to function in that role, and for members to agree on and accept the roles.

The following roles are recommended:

- Peer Facilitator
- Recorder
- Monitor: time and focus

Team Reflection: *Are the structures your school has in place for supporting teacher collaboration ensuring efficiency? Critical thinking? Collective action? If yes, what are the key components? If not, what structures are needed to ensure quality collaboration?*

NUTSHELL

Highly effective teacher teams are characterized by

- a learning network founded on common purpose and beliefs, relational trust, and an on-going communication system that supports sharing and building knowledge;
- practical and productive protocols to ensure meetings are efficient and focused on team-driven work; and
- structures that guarantee teams have the time and arrangements that support collaboration.

Understanding impact and responding strategically is what Impact Teams do. This transparent collaborative process deepens learning, alters perspective, and demands greater attention to alternate and possibly more effective ways of teaching and learning. Teachers build their knowledge by learning together and collective action strengthens their belief in their capacity to make a difference. This teaming builds collective teacher efficacy.

CHECK-IN

With your team, use the rubric below to reflect on the current state of teams. During your reflection, add ideas and next steps to enhance your collaborative practices.

Foundational Components	Not Yet	Sometimes	Always
Learning Network			
Team determines their common purpose (strengthening efficacy).			
Team identifies their common beliefs.			
Team assesses relational trust at least two times per year.			
Communication systems are established for transparent, consistent communication (cloud service).			

(Continued)

(Continued)

What's next?			
Foundational Components	**Not Yet**	**Sometimes**	**Always**
Process			
Protocols are followed based on the purpose of team meetings.			
Classroom protocols are used to enhance implementation of the formative assessment process.			
What's next?			
Foundational Components	**Not Yet**	**Sometimes**	**Always**
Structure			
Impact Teams meet weekly.			
Teams are configured to support common learning goals.			
Team roles are identified (facilitator, recorder, monitor).			
What's next?			

Teacher Voice

Brandi Landis, Third-Grade Teacher, Kelsey Norman Elementary, Joplin Schools

The work we have done with our Impact Team has changed the way I teach. My teaching partner and I meet regularly to norm our formative assessments as well as our summative assessment. We discuss not only where our students are in their learning progression and how well they understand a concept, but WHY they are where they are. We ask questions that help us discover why our students who have mastered a concept were able to master it, and ask what knowledge they have that others lack. Completing this step of our impact team meetings has had the greatest impact on my teaching.

Before impact teams, it never occurred to me to figure out the "root cause" of student success. In the past, I had only looked at information and skills students lacked.

Together my teaching partner and I develop strategies that we implement immediately. If she sees growth in her students that I don't see in my own, we look deeper into how each of us taught our lessons and share what worked well along with what was less effective. We are able to give each other ideas to try in our classrooms. We have seen positive gains in our students' learning as well as our own.

EFFICACY CONNECTIONS

- Effective dynamic collaboration leads to collective teacher efficacy (Siciliano, 2016).
- Teachers connected to peers with high levels of teacher self-efficacy will develop higher efficacy beliefs (Siciliano, 2016).
- Sharing knowledge is positively associated with teacher self-efficacy (Siciliano, 2016).

VIDEO DESCRIPTIONS

Chapter 3: Teaming to Learn

Overview: The videos in this chapter illustrate how instructional leaders and teacher teams refocused their traditional PLC structures to be truly centered on student learning.

	Video 3-1: Principal and Division Chair Interview, Lyons Township High School	Dr. Brian Waterman, principal of Lyons Township High School, and Karen Raino, Division Chair, discuss the power of purposeful protocols to ensure that student learning is emphasized during Impact Team meetings.
	Video 3-2: Teacher and Principal Testimonials, Reeds Spring School District	Susi Mauldin, Grade 6 communication arts teacher, talks about impact of the ITM.
	Video 3-3: Teaching and Learning Coach, Kelsey Norman Elementary, Joplin, MO	Hope Strasser, Teaching and Learning Coach, talks about how collaboration supports classroom clarity.
	Video 3-4: Principal Testimonial, Julie Munn, Kelsey Norman Elementary, Joplin, MO	Julie Munn, principal, talks about the ease of the EAA Team Meeting Protocol—Analyzing Student Work.

Strengthening Student Efficacy

4

The Formative Assessment Process in Action

"Assessment for learning happens in the classroom and involves students in every aspect of their own assessment to build their confidence and to maximize their achievement."

Stiggins & Chappuis, 2006

Mastery Moment: Describe the best experience you have had in helping students set goals and achieve them? What conditions were in place that led to your success?

THE WHAT: FORMATIVE ASSESSMENT UNPACKED

Quality formative assessment that involves students in every aspect of their own assessment utilizes pedagogies that are effective in strengthening student efficacy. The benefits of strengthening student efficacy are well documented (Margolis & McCabe, 2006). Students with a strong sense of efficacy are more likely to challenge themselves with difficult tasks and be intrinsically motivated. Students with strong efficacy will put forth a higher degree of effort to meet their goals, and they tend to attribute failure to factors that are in their control rather than blaming external factors. Self-efficacious students also recover quickly from mistakes and ultimately are more likely to achieve their goals. The Impact Team Model (ITM) utilizes quality formative assessment to create learning-focused relationships with students.

Formative assessment is a process not a product! It is not a single event or even a strategy. Stiggins (2007) states that assessment for learning happens in the classroom and involves students *in every aspect of their own assessment* to build their confidence and maximize their achievement. The role of the student as partner in the assessment process differentiates formative assessment from most other types of assessment. Black and William (1998) described formative assessment as

> all those activities undertaken by teachers, and by their students in assessing themselves, which provide information to be used as feedback to modify the teaching and learning activities in which they are engaged. Such assessment becomes "formative assessment" when the evidence is actually used to adapt the teaching work to meet the needs. (p. 2)

Nationally, formative assessment has been misunderstood. It has been thought of as an add-on or something extra after teaching has occurred. In actuality, formative assessment *is* learning and *is* effective teaching. Typically, students have not been involved in the formative assessment process. It is something teachers have done *to* them and not *with* them. Students involved in the formative assessment process are able to

- Compare their work to models of success;
- Self- and peer assess accurately;
- Use feedback to monitor and accelerate their learning;
- Give quality, accurate feedback to peers and the teacher;
- Set realistic, accurate learning goals; and
- Reflect on their learning and learn from their mistakes.

5 Core Practices

National and international researchers have identified five core practices of quality formative assessment (Heritage, 2008):

1. A classroom culture in which students and teachers are partners in learning is crucial. A high degree of relational trust must be established for learning to flourish.

2. Learning goals and/or intentions and criteria for success are clearly identified and communicated to students.

3. Learning progressions clearly articulate the subgoals of the ultimate learning goal.

4. Students are provided with evidence-based feedback that is linked to the criteria for success.

5. Both self- and peer assessment are important for providing students the opportunity to think metacognitively about their learning.

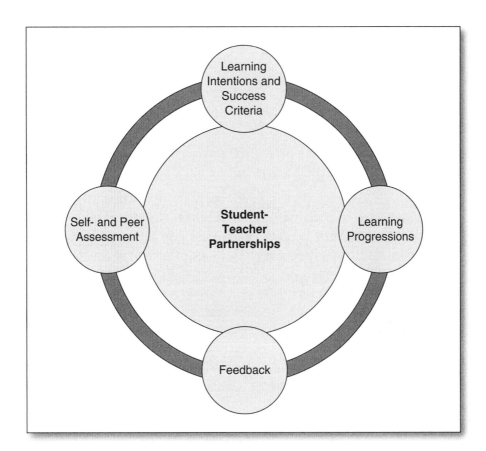

Core Practice 1: Learning-Focused Relationships

The student-teacher partnership is at the core of the formative assessment process. Without this partnership, formative assessment falls flat! It is crucial for teachers and students to develop learning-focused relationships. Formative assessment puts students at the center. It promotes and gives first priority to students understanding their learning.

Core Practice 2: Learning Intentions and Success Criteria

The first step in the formative assessment process is to define the overarching learning goals or *learning intention* for the cycle of learning. The ultimate learning intention is represented by district priority standards that are determined from the state standards. Learning intentions are written in student-friendly language so students clearly understand the goal for learning.

Teachers develop overarching learning intentions that focus their learning cycles. They then develop their daily learning intentions based on the progression of learning (content) and strategies (process) that teachers teach so students master the standard. Daily learning intentions or teaching points are responsive to student needs and are written in student-friendly language. It important to note that the teaching point or daily learning intention doesn't change daily, because students need time to practice and get feedback. Practice makes perfect!

Success criteria describe successful attainment of the learning intention.

Sometimes success criteria are referred to as *look-fors*. Success criteria help students understand what to look for during the learning and what it looks like once they have learned. Quality success criteria make the learning clear for students and teachers alike. Success criteria can be illustrated best with students when: using exemplars, creating worked examples with students, analyzing samples of strong and weak work, and having students identify success criteria in the latter examples. Ultimately they identify the significant aspects of student performance that are assessed and tested related to curriculum expectations. Success criteria are directly connected to a product or performance (e.g., discussion, a written task, a diagram, etc.). Success criteria can be process based and/or content based.

Example

Overarching learning intention:

> *We are learning to determine main ideas and supporting details in text.*

Daily learning intention:

> *Today we are learning to create and complete a graphic organizer that illustrates the main idea and supporting details of an article.*

Success Criteria:

- *Create an organizer that organizes your thinking (main idea and key details).*
- *Write a main idea statement—place appropriately in your organizer.*
- *Paraphrase at least three strong key details that support the main idea— place appropriately in your organizer.*

Once teachers have collaboratively determined the success criteria for a given product or performance, the success criteria need to be communicated to students. Collaboratively examining student work, exemplars, and creating worked examples *with* students are effective strategies for teachers to begin to communicate or co-construct the success criteria for a task or activity aligned to unit or lesson learning intentions. Although this may take substantial time in classrooms to define the success criteria, there are tremendous benefits. Shepard (2006) explains:

> [W]hen teachers help students to understand and internalize the standards of excellence in a discipline—that is, what makes a good history paper or a good mathematical explanation—they are helping them develop metacognitive awareness about what they need to attend to as they are writing or problem solving. Indeed, learning the rules and forms of a discipline is part of learning the discipline, not just a means to systematize or justify grading. (p. 631)

Core Practice 3: Learning Progressions

Teachers and students utilize learning progressions to determine the focus or overarching learning intention for their learning cycle. Learning progressions clarify the pathway that students are expected to progress in a domain. The progression identifies the knowledge and skills that students need to meet to reach the overarching learning goal. The progression also defines the prerequisite knowledge and skills as well as a pathway for future learning.

CCSS Learning Progression Example: Reading for Literature Anchor 2

Grade Level 2	Grade Level 3	Grade Level 4	Grade Level 5
Identify the main topic of a multi-paragraph text.	Determine the main idea of the text.	Determine the main idea of the text.	Determine two or more main ideas of a text.
	May infer main idea from key details	May infer main idea from key details	May infer main idea(s) from key details
Identify the specific focus of specific paragraphs within the text.	Recount the key details. Explain how they support the main idea.	Explain how the main idea is supported by key details.	Explain how main ideas are supported by key details.
		Summarize the text.	Summarize the text.

Teachers develop their daily learning intentions or teaching points based on the overarching learning intentions using the learning progression to support scaffolding and differentiated instruction. In addition, teachers teach students strategies or approaches to access and master the standard. A deep understanding of the learning progression allows teachers to scaffold the learning for students. The progression gives teachers a defined pathway that ultimately supports them in making decisions that are best for individual students.

The rate of individual students' progress may vary along the learning progressions, but progressions should ultimately connect the knowledge, concepts, and skills students develop as they evolve from novice to more expert performances (Heritage, 2008). This gives teachers and students an explicit pathway for learning. Feedback based on the success criteria provides both teachers and students with descriptive and constructive information on exactly where the student is in relation to the learning goal. Teachers and students should be able to see and understand the scaffolding they will be climbing as they approach (Stiggins, 2005, p. 327) the overarching learning intention or goal. In addition, if learning is derailed at any point, a teacher and student can identify the misconception and then make midcourse corrections.

Overarching and daily learning intentions or goals are the critical first steps in the implementation of the formative assessment process. Research around goal orientation indicates that students are more likely to be "challenge seekers" than "challenge avoiders" (Meyer, Turner, & Spencer, 1997) when motivated by progress. The specific expectations set forth in state and national standards describe what students should know and be able to do at the end of the grade.

Usually the standards need to be expressed in grade-appropriate, student-friendly language and/or broken down into smaller increments, particularly when differentiating to address diverse learning needs and levels of student readiness.

Core Practice 4: Evidence-Based Feedback

The formative assessment process is really *all about* feedback. For deep implementation to occur, feedback must be integrated into all components of the formative assessment process. Feedback is reciprocal: feedback to the student from the teacher, from the student to the teacher, from and to peers, from and to self.

So what does *good feedback* look like? Sound like? Feel like? First, we need to define feedback. Effective feedback provides critical information about where the student is in relation to the learning goal and what they need to learn next. The litmus test of effective feedback is when a student is able to answer the three feedback questions:

1. Where am I going? (Feed-up)

2. Where am I in the learning? (Feed-back)

3. What do I need to learn next? (Feed-forward)

Since Black and Wiliam (1998) published their seminal research, *Inside the Black Box*, identifying feedback as a way to double the rate of student learning, feedback has been recognized as being integral to student success. Effective feedback is directly connected to what criteria or competencies the student needs to know and do in relationship to mastering school and district priority standards. Nicol and Macfarlane-Dick (2005) list seven principles of good feedback practice:

1. It clarifies what good performance is (goals, criteria, expected standards).

2. It facilitates the development of self-assessment in learning.

3. It provides high quality information to students about their learning.

4. It encourages teacher and peer dialogue around learning.

5. It encourages positive motivational beliefs and self-esteem.

6. It provides opportunities to close the gap between current and desired performance.

7. It provides information to teachers that can be used to help shape teaching. (p. 1)

To give and/or receive feedback with openness and as an opportunity to progress, a classroom culture of trust must be created. Feeling safe allows for the feedback to be heard. Reciprocal feedback is the *heart and soul* of the formative assessment process. Feedback "lives" in all the Impact Team Model Purposeful Protocols.

Core Practice 5: Self-Assessment, Peer Assessment, and Goal Setting

Students must be taught how to self- and peer assess and to set goals. Therefore, teachers must model using think aloud during these core practices. Rollheiser and Ross (2000) describe a four-stage model for teaching students to self- and peer assess.

Stage 1: Define together with students the success criteria that will be used to assess their learning.

Stage 2: Teach students how to apply the criteria. This can be done successfully through explaining and modeling using a sample of student work.

Stage 3: Give students descriptive feedback on the quality of their self- and peer assessments. This means that teachers have to confer with students and give feedback to lift the level of peer-to-peer feedback.

Stage 4: Partner with students to develop individual learning goals and action plans.

Teachers must conference frequently with students to ensure that self- and peer assessment is accurate and reliable. Teachers must give feedback to students on the feedback students give to each other to ensure reliability; this is called feedback on feedback. *Feedback on feedback* is crucial to the success of quality self- and peer assessment. Although this takes time, it is time well spent.

After students have received feedback from self- and peer assessment, they set learning goals. Students take the following actions to ensure that feedback is received from their peers, teacher, and self:

- Create individual learning goals and/or action plans.
- Collect student work in an e-portfolio to show progress and mastery for focus standards.
- Revise their work to demonstrate that they have used the evidence-based feedback to progress in their learning.
- Reflect on their learning using evidence-based feedback to determine their strengths and next learning steps.

It is crucial that teachers explicitly model for students how to take action based on the feedback they have received from their peers and their teacher. Teachers model how to set learning goals for students and give evidence-based feedback about the reliability and validity of student learning goals. Teachers hold students accountable for the goals they set and guide students to monitor goals for themselves. In addition, teachers model how to reflect on their goals, monitor their goals, revise their goals, and make midcourse corrections when the need arises.

Short-Term Goals: Students use the success criteria for the assignment or assessment task to create individual, short-term, learning goals. Students highlight any criterion they did not meet and use the criterion to set individual learning goals.

Long-Term Goals: Students analyze how they are doing overall in a course or subject in relationship to the short-term goals they create. They may use unit-based learning targets to take stock of how they are doing overall in relationship to what they are supposed to learn in that particular unit. Again, students must be explicitly taught how to do this. Teachers use think aloud regularly and model for students how to do this and then gradually release responsibility to the students. This will result in ongoing coaching and feedback to ensure that students are creating effective individual learning goals.

THE WHY: RESEARCH AND REASONS

Reason 1: This practice increases confidence and self-efficacy. Confidence and efficacy play a role in meaningful self-assessment and goal setting. Ross (2006) points out that when teachers explicitly teach students how to set appropriate goals and assess their work accurately, teachers can promote an upward cycle of learning and self-confidence. When students demonstrate mastery, self-efficacy is strengthened.

Reason 2: This practice increases achievement. Meta-analysis of studies into formative assessment have indicated significant learning gains across all content areas, knowledge and skill types, and levels of education when formative assessment is used. Terrance Crooks (1988) reports that effects sizes for summative assessments are consistently lower than effect sizes for formative assessments.

Hattie's (2009) synthesis on self-reported grading/student expectations reported a 1.44 effect on the learning. This effect translates into over 3 years of learning in 1 year's time. This influence involves the teacher understanding what the student's expectations are. Then the teacher pushes the student to exceed those expectations. Once the student exceeds her own expectations, she gains confidence in her ability.

Reason 3: Formative assessment personalizes teaching. The formative assessment process allows the student-teacher partnership to determine what standards and/or competencies students already know and to what degree. Teachers and students can make decisions together regarding instructional next steps. In addition, teachers can create appropriate lessons and activities for groups of learners or individual students and then reassess.

Reason 4: Collaborative learning increases efficacy. Regularly engaging students in peer assessment gives students the ability to understand their own strengths and learning challenges. When students create learning goals and monitor their goals, it creates ownership of the learning. Owning the learning is key to engagement and motivation. Bandura (1994) also concludes that cooperative learning strategies have the dual outcome of improving both self-efficacy and academic achievement.

Reason 5: Students learn lifelong skills. Engaging students regularly in the formative assessment process supports their development of valuable lifelong skills such as self-evaluation and self-regulation. Specifically, *self-regulation* is defined as the capacity to alter behaviors. It enables people to adjust their actions in a wide range of social, situational, and academic demands (Baumeister & Vohs, 2007). Students learn what it takes to learn—perseverance, effort, and learning from mistakes.

THE HOW: THREE PURPOSEFUL PROTOCOLS

The ITM relies on three of the eight protocols to ensure fidelity of the formative assessment process into classroom culture.

- Evidence • Analysis • Action (EAA) Classroom
- Lesson Study
- Microteaching

We define *fidelity* as ensuring that students are involved in every aspect of the formative assessment process. The word *fidelity* does not imply that implementation of the process is linear or that every teacher has to implement the process in the exact same way. We have found that implementation is quite messy and since classroom management is key to the successful implementation of the process, implementation evolves differently from class to class. However, it is important that the five key components of formative assessment provide a foundation for implementation.

 ## EVIDENCE • ANALYSIS • ACTION (EAA) IN THE CLASSROOM

The ITM uses a classroom protocol (Evidence • Analysis • Action [EAA] Classroom) to operationalize the five core formative assessment practices. The classroom protocol has three phases:

1. Evidence
   - Learning Intentions
   - Success Criteria

2. Analysis
   - Self- and Peer Assessment
   - Feedback

3. Action
   - Goal Setting
   - Revision

The three phases combine to create a cycle of learning in which students and teachers partner together during each phase. Each phase of the protocol supports teachers in deep implementation of the formative assessment process. The length of each learning cycle is determined by curricular goals and student need. Impact Teams ensure that students know what they are expected to know, understand, and do by designing learning cycles in incremental steps to build student knowledge and skills.

Team Activity: With your team, use the EAA Classroom Rubric to assess the implementation of the formative assessment process. Go over each phase and component with your team. What components are you successfully implementing? What components do you need to focus on?

EAA Classroom Success Criteria (NY = *Not Yet, S = Sometimes, U = Usually*)	NY	S	U
(1) EVIDENCE			
Learning Intentions (LI) and Success Criteria (SC)			
Teacher explains and models using samples of student work or exemplars to illustrate the success criteria of the perspective product or performance.			
Students can articulate the learning intention and success criteria.			
Students engage in co-construction of the success criteria with their classmates and teacher.			
Students can identify success criteria in student work samples and exemplars.			
Students reflect regularly using essential questions connected to big ideas.			
Assessment Tools			
Rubrics and or checklists reflect the learning intention and success criteria aligned to focus learning progression/standard(s).			
Exemplars are annotated by the success criteria and are visible to students (notebooks, learning management system [LMS], classroom environment).			
Samples of student work are used so students can practice applying the success criteria (varying degrees of proficiency).			

(Continued)

(Continued)

EAA Classroom Success Criteria (NY = *Not Yet*, S = *Sometimes*, U = *Usually*)	NY	S	U
(2) ANALYSIS			
Peer and Self-Assessment, Feedback			
Teacher models how to self- and peer assess using samples of student work. Teacher thinks aloud while modeling the process.			
Teacher models how to give and receive evidence-based feedback in a respectful manner. Feedback language stems and frames are posted for students to use during this process.			
Students use rubrics and/or checklists when engaged in self-assessment and peer assessment.			
Students get regular practice applying the success criteria.			
Students can identify success criteria in other's work.			
Students can give feedback based on the success criteria in a respectful manner.			
Students engage in reflective dialogue with peers and teacher based on rubrics and/or checklist.			
Students get regular feedback from teacher to lift the accuracy of their self- and peer assessments.			
(3) ACTION			
Goal Setting, Revision, Feedback			
Teacher models how to set learning goals, make action plans, revise student work, and reflect using evidence-based feedback.			
Students reflect on their strengths and next steps based on feedback from peer and self-assessment and teacher.			
Students create personal learning goals based on feedback.			
Students revise assessment product based on feedback tied to rubric and/or checklist.			
Students keep track of their progress and mastery of Focus Standards (they have a way to organize their learning).			

Modeling Each Component: It is important to note the importance of explaining and modeling each of the five practices of the formative assessment process with students. Think aloud is an important strategy to use while modeling so students can get a window into the thinking of the learner. All the components of the formative assessment process must be modeled and taught to students.

Teachers can model each component or attribute using anonymous samples of student work or they use a sample of work they coconstruct with the students in class. Teachers gradually release responsibility and then provide constant feedback and coaching to ensure each phase of the classroom protocol is done with fidelity to ensure reliability and validity of students' peer and self-assessments and students' learning goals and action plans. Students must explicitly be taught each component of the process.

EAA Classroom Protocol: Description

(1) **EVIDENCE**: Three components of the formative assessment process are introduced during the first phase of the EAA protocol.

- Learning Intentions and co-construction of success criteria
- Learning progressions
- Evidence-based feedback

This phase is the most important phase in the classroom. During this phase expectations are set *with* students. When implementing the formative assessment process, students and teachers must have a crystal clear understanding about what is expected and what quality work or evidence looks like. The evidence can be co-constructed through inquiry, can be modeled from the teacher, can be modeled from other students, or can be determined by analyzing examples of strong and weak work so that students and teachers come up with a shared understanding of what proficiency is.

(2) **ANALYSIS:** The two components of the formative assessment process that are operationalized during this phase of the EAA protocol are

- self-assessment and peer assessment and
- evidence-based feedback.

During this phase, students analyze their work through the lens of the learning intention and success criteria. Success criteria are embedded in either a checklist or a rubric. The assessment criteria on the rubric are directly aligned to the standards and provide evidence of student learning.

The Ladder of Feedback: Typically teachers develop classroom norms to ensure that students are giving constructive and respectful evidence-based feedback. The "Ladder of Feedback" (Perkins, 2003) is a protocol or structure that establishes a classroom culture of trust. The Ladder of Feedback guides students through four steps:

1. Clarification

2. Values

3. Concerns

4. Suggestions

The first step of the ladder gives the reviewer (Student A) a chance to ask the assessed (Student B) clarifying questions about the student work. In Step 2, Student A identifies something they value in Student B's work to help him or her build on strengths. During Step 3 of the ladder, Student B raises concerns. During Step 4, the reviewer makes suggestions for improvement. These suggestions are feedback and should offer Student B some ideas on next steps.

Before this protocol, the teacher models this process for students. It is important to note that sentence stems and phrases should be brainstormed for each phase of the process to ensure that students develop a language for evidence-based feedback.

Possible Feedback Stems:

1. Clarify:
   - What would you like me to focus on during our review?
   - Can you describe what you wanted to learn?
   - Help me understand what you wanted to convey.

2. Value:
   - I thought this was very effective . . .
   - I appreciate the way you illustrate . . .
   - This worked very well . . .

3. Concern:
   - I wonder if . . .
   - It seems to me that . . .

4. Suggest:
   - What if . . .
   - Maybe you could . . .
   - Another idea may be to . . .

Note: Ladder of Feedback in Appendix A-9

(3) **ACTION:** During the action phase of the EAA classroom proto-col, students are taught to take action based on the evidence-based feedback given during peer and self-assessment. Goal setting and revision are key components to effective implementation of the formative assessment process into classroom culture. Teachers partner with students to ensure that goal setting is not a separate event that has little connection to what students are learning. Teachers must explain and model effective goal setting and give students ample opportunities to practice goal setting. Students must be given feedback on the goals they set so they learn how to set and monitor their goals.

Gregory, Cameron, and Davies (2011) suggest a 1- to 3-month period to give students a reasonable length of time to make noticeable improvement. They suggest three ways to help students set learning goals:

1. Break down general goals into manageable pieces with students

2. Model how to fill out goal setting planning frames so students can see how using a frame can help them set goals

3. Have students interview one another about their learning goals so students can clarify and revise their goals if necessary

Planning Frame Example:

To make progress at _____ I could . . .

How I plan to do this is . . .

I will do this by _____

I will know I am successful by using the following evidence:

Peer Interview Example:

> 1. Can you accomplish your goal?
>
> 2. How did you determine the time frame to accomplish your goal?
>
> 3. How will you know you are making progress?
>
> 4. What evidence are you using to show others that you are making progress?
>
> 5. Explain the models of success you are using to help you achieve your goal.
>
> 6. Who do you think could help you reach your goal?

Note: Planning Frames in Appendix A-10

James wanted to empower students to own their learning in his freshman level World History Class. He used the EAA Classroom Protocol as a guide for successful implementation of the formative assessment process. The class has to answer the following essential question using the BEAST Writing Rubric (Appendix C-6) that the World History Impact Team coconstructed the previous summer.

Essential Question: Was Ancient Mesopotamia a civilized or uncivilized place to live?

James Milkert, Lyons Township High School, IL

Read the following transcription. Pay close attention to each part of the EAA Classroom Protocol. The transcription is based on a 50-minute class period.

(1) EVIDENCE

Coconstructing Success Criteria

James*:*   *Today is a big day. The goal that we are going to work on today we are going to work on for the rest of the year. We will get there. It is going to be a challenge, but we are going to work hard and become great historians by the end of the year. Today we are going to use ROCKSTAR success criteria for two parts of our BEAST writing rubric:* **Evidence and Analysis**.

Today we are going to co-construct the criteria for these two sections of our rubric. We will discuss it together, just like we did with the **Big Idea** *category from our rubric. We will talk about what "rockstar" criteria looks like and how to do it. And then we will practice this week to get as close as we can.*

Brainstorm at your tables what you need to be successful for the EVIDENCE section and ANALYSIS section of our BEAST writing rubric.

Students: *Students discussed the criteria in table groups*

James: *So what do you need to be successful on our rubric?*

Students:

- *We need to know how to get evidence.*
- *We need to know what evidence is credible or not.*
- *We need to know what sources to look at first for credible evidence.*

James: *Why is that important?*

Students: *If we make a claim, we have to have credible, reliable evidence to back it up.*

James: *What else do we need to be successful?*

Students:

- *We need to know what the criteria means.*
- *We have to assess the credibility of the evidence.*
- *We have to be able to explain how the evidence supports our claim or big idea.*

James: *Yes, we need to be able to analyze the evidence, or explain how the evidence supports our rubric. What are we trying to prove in our writing?*

Students:

- *We are trying to prove our point.*
- *We need to know a lot about the topic so we can back up our big idea or claim.*

James: *Yes, that is perfect. We have to have credible evidence AND a lot of it to back up our claim.*

(2) ANALYSIS

Modeling Peer Assessment

James: *Please take a blank Ladder of Feedback guide out and put it on your desk. You are going to complete one of these for a partner after you read their work. Practice with me first.*

(James shows an example of his own writing on the document camera.)

This is my writing. I wrote it. I am feeling really insecure about my work and I am feeling a little defensive about it because I am not sure if it is any good. So take it easy on me. The way we give feedback is we start positive. What do you value about my work? You can use the feedback stems located in the template, if you want.

Students: *I like how you put all the effort into your work. I can tell you worked hard on it.*

James: *Thank you for noticing, I stayed up late, and I worked really hard on this! Now I am listening to you because you noticed something of value related to my work. Okay now go to the next section of the template. Do you have any clarifying questions for me?*

Students: *Help me understand why you chose the facts you chose as the evidence.*

James: *I chose these facts because they were from a primary source. They are credible facts, and they back up my claim. Okay, now give me a suggestion. I get the feeling you don't feel very good about my work. What suggestion can you give me? You can use the sentence stems or come up with a suggestion on your own. What can I do next time to improve?*

Students: *Be more descriptive with your analyzing.*

James: *I am not sure what you mean. What does that mean to be more descriptive? If I have to analyze, what do I have to do?*

Students: *You have to go over it, and you have to explain the evidence.*

James: *Okay, so I have to explain the evidence better. I can do that.*

Scaffolding Peer Assessment

James: *Okay now you have 3 minutes to read over your partner's work and compare it to the model on the screen. Notice how I put the evidence in one color and the analysis in another color. Read your partner's work and highlight each section of the rubric in another color. Then use the Ladder of Feedback Guide to give your partner feedback. You have 3 minutes.*

Students: *Students read a partner's work and highlighted the evidence in one color and analysis in another color. They then gave feedback to a partner on the template.*

James: *Okay, now talk with your partner. You have 3 minutes each. Give your partner some positive specific feedback and then give them at least one suggestion. (James then listened in to each partnership and gave them feedback on their feedback; James took notes on the validity and reliability of students' peer-to-peer feedback.)*

James: *(James sits with two girls and listens in on their conversation.) What did you say you liked?*

Student 1: *I liked how she used evidence to sound like she knew what she's talking about.*

James: *What part?*

Student 1: *Right here when she talked about trading, she included everything they traded.*

James: *Did you hear that, that is a compliment. What did she say?*

Student 2: *She liked how I used a lot of examples to back up my claim about trading.*

James: *That is good. That is very good. You used a lot of evidence and gave examples. Does she tell you what civilized looks like in her mind? Can you visualize "civilized."*

Student 1: *No, actually that is something that she needs to work on. She needs to give more examples about the ancient people being civilized.*

(3) ACTION

Modeling and Scaffolding Goal Setting

James: *I can set a goal for myself based on the feedback I get from my friends. Let me show you what I mean. Take a look at the screen. Here is a goal for myself. What do you think? Talk with a partner.*

Students: *It isn't very good. There are no details.*

James: *That is correct. I have to use the success criteria from the rubric to create specific goals that are measurable. Now take a look at this goal. (James puts an exemplar goal on the screen.) How is this different than my first goal?*

Students*:*   *It is specific and very detailed. You used the success criteria in your goals, and you explained what you had to do to be successful in reaching your goal.*

James*:*   *Great. Now you try. You have 3 minutes to write a goal using the template provided. I will walk around and give you feedback on your goals.*

Team Activity: Read the classroom transcription with a teammate. Identify the criteria from each phase of the EAA Classroom Rubric in the transcription. What evidence can you find that illustrates that James is implementing the formative assessment process with his students?

What is similar or different from how you engage students in the formative assessment process?

 Read about PS 9's journey implementing the EAA Classroom Protocol into primary classrooms written by Deanna Marco, founding principal of PS 9 in Staten Island, New York.

As a PreK–2 school with only two to three classes on a grade level, consistency and vertical alignment was crucial. As a school, we began to brainstorm a system and common language that would make sense for students of all ages. The staff agreed to try out the stoplight system: Green—I got this; Yellow—I tried, but need some help; and Red—I need help. We began using this system across all structures of the school day including basic things such as line up, clean up, playtime, and so on. What we found was so surprising: Students, as young as 4 years old, were being really honest about their needs. The teachers quickly shifted the language into instruction by asking students to use the visual stoplight we created to self-assess themselves after a mini lesson and during independent work time, and again, students were reflective and truthful. Early on students began to realize that is was not only acceptable to need help, but also encouraged to express yourself when you do not understand something. Developing this trust with students set the tone for peer assessment.

As teachers gained greater understanding of the standards, they began to create rubrics and checklists using standards-based success criteria, which provided both the teachers and the students with clear expectations for their learning. We created a school-wide template for success criteria with the language of the stoplight system built into to the document to provide students with a familiar structure, format, and language across grade levels. We slowly began to model self-assessment with success criteria and exemplar pieces of work and invited students to do the same. Our language was simple: "What did you do well?" and "What are your next steps are?" We were amazed at how quickly students were able to identify their needs and saw a dramatic improvement in their work immediately. Admittedly, we went success criteria crazy!

Currently, our focus is on peer-assessment. Using success criteria and flexible partnerships, students work together to provide one another with a "Glow" and a "Grow." A *glow* is a statement of positive feedback, and a *grow* is a next step. Teachers co-constructed language stems to use when providing glows and grows. Peer assessment has made a profound change in student work products. Our biggest discovery is that student work is remarkably improved when they know their peers are giving them feedback.

My journey with self- and peer assessment began just about a year ago. This work has transformed the way my teachers plan for instruction and their approach to feedback. There is a level of trust amongst students and teachers that has inspired us to keep moving on this journey.

Rubric-Bound Assessment Examples in Appendix-C

LESSON STUDY PROTOCOL

Impact Teams use lesson study to improve instructional effectiveness specific to the formative assessment process. It is a collaborative learning process in which teacher teams examine their practice from the planning stage through teaching, observing, and critiquing. The team creates a detailed lesson plan which one teacher teaches and the others observe. The focus of the observation is on the students' responses rather than the teacher's actions. Based on the evidence, the team revises the lesson. The teachers can then go and teach the lesson another time after making the appropriate adjustments.

Time

- 45–60 minutes for developing lessons
- 30–60 minutes for observing lessons
- 40–60 minutes for analyzing and refining lesson

Resources

- curricular materials for lesson development
- release time for team members to observe lesson
- projection (if possible)

Materials

- Copy of lesson plan, template for recording observation—teacher actions and student responses

Step	Procedure	Time Allotment
1	**Lesson Planning**	45–60 minutes
	<ul><li>Team plans lesson to observe</li><li>Team agrees on the teacher actions/strategies</li><li>Team reaches consensus on the intended student behaviors for each teacher action (observable behaviors)</li><li>Team identifies possible difficulties students might have</li><li>Team determines the intervention for each difficulty</li><li>Team constructs observation template that has agreed-upon teacher actions identified with a space to record student behaviors for each teacher action</li></ul>	
2	**Evidence: Team Observation**	30–60 minutes
	<ul><li>Team uses observation template to record student behaviors</li><li>Team does not interact with students</li><li>This can be recorded if classroom coverage is not available</li></ul>	
3	**Analysis: Lesson Analysis**	40–60 minutes
	<ul><li>Teams use the evidence of student behaviors to analyze what parts of the lesson were effective (why?)</li><li>Teams use the evidence of student behaviors to analyze what parts of the lesson were ineffective (why not?)</li></ul>	
4	**Action: Lesson Refinement**	10–20 minutes
	<ul><li>Team refines the lesson based on the analysis</li></ul>	

))) LESSON STUDY IN ACTION BY CAROL CRONK

Problem of Practice

One of the greatest struggles is to support the building of a mathematics lesson that measures what the teachers are expecting the students to learn. Lessons are frequently not as focused and not as successful as was intended. This is despite the fact that lessons were designed backwards from the learning intention(s) to creating the end of lesson task, to working out the task, and then discussing the outcomes and creating a scoring guide/rubric for the task.

The Solution

After creating a lesson to be taught to a specific group of students, and so much articulation about the learning intention and measuring student progress, the teachers still seemed to have trouble communicating to the students what they were supposed to learn from the lesson. We would plan for that communication to happen, but it simply failed to happen that way.

1. This year we decided to build not only learning intentions into the lesson plan but also the success criteria. This seems to be the piece that is missing.

2. As the development of the lesson progresses, we refer back to the unpacked learning intentions and success criteria to see if we are staying on track.

3. In addition, the table with the learning intentions and success criteria is part of the information provided explicitly to the students along with the mathematical task.

Our Impact

Teachers are remembering to communicate the learning intentions to the students and the *students* have a much better idea of what they are supposed to be learning during the lesson. In addition, the focus on the lesson is more streamlined and student exit cards show better conceptual understanding by the students.

The example below is from a group of high school teachers who are concerned about freshmen with gaps in their understanding. The lesson associated with these learning intentions is one of a set of lessons that include *number talks* and *close reading* taught to students during the first 2 weeks of school.

Learning Intentions	Success Criteria
• *Describe distributive property in your own words* • *Give an example of distributive property* • *Write and solve a numerical expression (distributive property) from a contextual situation* • *Change numeric expression to algebraic expression and solve*	• *Accurately describe distributive property "multiplying everything inside the () by number outside"* • *Provide contextual (preferred) or numerical expression (acceptable)* • *2($5+$3)=$16* • *Represent a word problem as a numerical expression and solve 2(x+3)=16* • *Change a numerical expression to a algebraic expression and solve*

Carol Cronk is currently a partner consultant for The Core Collaborative specializing in leading Impact Teams. She is a codirector for the Inland Counties Mathematics Project in California and previously served as the K–12 Mathematics Coordinator at the San Bernardino County Superintendent of Schools.

Activity: How would your team use the Lesson Study protocol to work on a problem of practice regarding implementing the formative assessment process?

Brainstorm a list with your team about what you would focus on using the Lesson Study Protocol.

MICROTEACHING PROTOCOL

Microteaching is organized practice teaching that provides Impact Team members the opportunity to try out small parts of lessons and/or strategies specific to the formative assessment process and receive constructive feedback for improvement. The mini lessons are recorded prior to the Impact Team meetings based on a strategy or approach that the team wants to learn—this need comes up typically while the team is using the EAA Meeting Protocol. The team observes the video and provides feedback to the practice teacher. Then each member of the team has an opportunity to try the technique observed. The team then summarizes what was learned after the session.

Time

- 45–50 minutes

Resources

- Mini-lesson preparation by the "practice teacher"
- Video Recording

Materials

- Identified focus for feedback (criteria) / EAA Classroom Protocol

Step	Procedure	Minutes
1	**Evidence • Video Observation**	
	• Team determines "lens" for observation • Criteria from the EAA Classroom Protocol can provide a lens for observation • Team observes "practice teacher" engaging students in a specific formative assessment practice • Team takes notes in connection with the criteria used for observing	5–10
2	**Analysis**	
	Appreciative Feedback	5
	• Team names specific strengths associated with criteria for observation	
	Self-Assessment and Clarification	5–10
	• Practice teacher reflects on the lesson after appreciative feedback • Reflection may include strengths and possible next steps • Team asks clarifying questions prior to team practice	
3	**Action**	
	Team Practice	10
	• Team members practice the strategy observed with a partner or triad based on a future unit • Each team member gets an opportunity to practice	
	Feedback Summary	5–10
	• Team collaboratively identifies one or two ways to improve teaching technique based on practice and feedback	

MICROTEACHING IN ACTION

The English Department chair wanted to build capacity in her building regarding student goal setting with the English 3 Team. The English 3 lead teacher had just volunteered for a coaching connected to the power of think aloud and using examples when modeling the core practices of assessment for learning.

The English 3 lead teacher recorded herself guiding students with peer review in her English class. The team observed the video together and then analyzed the video to determine strengths and possible next steps for how they would use the strategy in their own classrooms. They then had a few moments to practice with a colleague before they actually taught it with their own students.

ACTIVITY

Read the Impact Team Microteaching Notes with your team. How would you use this protocol with your team? What component of the formative assessment process would benefit from microteaching?

Microteaching Note Template

Evidence • Observation Criteria
Teacher: Clarify the evidence. Describe the approach and the criteria for success.
The teacher used think aloud to model using the ladder of feedback with her English class. The teacher adapted the feedback ladder to include: • *Value* • *Clarify* • *Suggestions*
Analysis • Name Strengths
Team: What was effective? Why was it effective?
• The think aloud was very clear • The students writing down the steps to using the ladder of feedback thought it was effective; they could use the model to support the process • The template was effective, it had effective sentence stems for the students • The students were engaged because they were filling in a blank template
Teacher: Would you continue to use this approach? Why? What would you change if you did it again?
Yes, the template worked really well. I would break up the process more and allow the students to talk more in between.

> **Action • Practice and Summary**
>
> **Team: How would you turnkey this approach in your classroom? How would you adapt this to fit your needs?**
>
> *Each teacher shared with a partner how he or she would adapt it to fit where they were at in the curriculum. They did this in teams.*
>
> **Team: What did we learn from this experience?**
>
> *Think aloud is very important when teaching peer review. We need to model each step and not assume the students know what to do.*

NUTSHELL

There are five core formative assessment practices. A learning focused relationship is developed when students are involved in all aspects of the formative assessment process. Implementing the formative assessment process uses pedagogies that also increase efficacy: collaborative learning, goal setting, self- and peer assessment, reflection, action planning.

The ITM utilizes three classroom-based protocols that support teachers in implementing the formative assessment process successfully in classroom instruction. Quality formative assessment *is* effective teaching.

CHECK-IN

Use the rubric below to assess your system or individual classroom to determine where you are at in implementation of the formative assessment process. There is a section labeled "next steps" after each category on the rubric; use this space to create goals for each section. What evidence would you collect to justify your reasoning?

EAA Classroom Success Criteria *(NY=Not Yet, S=Sometimes, U=Usually)*	NY	S	U
(1) EVIDENCE			
Learning Intentions (LI) and Success Criteria (SC)			
Teacher explains and models using samples of student work or exemplars to illustrate the success criteria of the perspective product or performance.			
Students can articulate the learning intention and success criteria.			

(Continued)

(Continued)

EAA Classroom Success Criteria (NY=*Not Yet, S=Sometimes, U=Usually*)	NY	S	U
Students engage in coconstruction of the success criteria with their classmates and teacher.			
Students can identify success criteria in student work samples and exemplars.			
Students reflect regularly using essential questions connected to big ideas.			
Assessment Tools			
Formative assessments reflect the learning intention and success criteria aligned to focus learning progression/standard(s) (rubrics/checklists)			
Exemplars are annotated by the success criteria and are visible to students (notebooks, LMS, classroom environment)			
Samples of student work are used so students can practice applying the success criteria (varying degrees of proficiency)			
Next Steps:			
(2) ANALYSIS			
Peer and Self-Assessment, Feedback			
Teacher models how to self- and peer assess using samples of student work. Teacher thinks aloud while modeling the process.			
Teacher models how to give and receive evidence-based feedback in a respectful manner. Feedback language stems and frames are posted for students to use during this process.			
Students use rubrics and/or checklists when engaged in self-assessment and peer assessment.			

EAA Classroom Success Criteria (NY=*Not Yet*, S=*Sometimes*, U=*Usually*)	NY	S	U
Students get regular practice applying the SC.			
Students can identify SC in others' work.			
Students can give feedback based on the SC in a respectful manner.			
Students engage in reflective dialogue with peers and teacher based on rubrics and/or checklists.			
Students get regular feedback from teacher to lift the accuracy of their self- and peer assessments.			
Next Steps:			

(3) ACTION			
Goal Setting, Revision, Feedback			
Teacher models how to set learning goals, make action plans, revise student work. and reflect using evidence-based feedback.			
Students reflect on their strengths and next steps based on feedback from peer and self-assessment and teacher.			
Students create personal learning goals based on feedback.			
Students revise assessment based on feedback tied to rubric and/or checklist.			
Students keep track of their progress and mastery of Focus Standards (they have a way to organize their learning).			
Next Steps:			

Activity:

Teachers can leverage the four sources of efficacy purposefully by engaging students regularly in the formative assessment process.

Complete the table with your team. What are some examples of the formative assessment five core practices that leverage the four sources of efficacy? One example has been provided for each source.

4 Sources of Efficacy	Classroom Examples
Mastery Moments	● Meeting a learning goal ● ●
Models of Success	● Utilizing exemplars ● ●
Feedback	● Feedback tied to success criteria ● ●
Safety	● Modeling learning from mistakes ● ●

EFFICACY CONNECTIONS

- Comparing student performance to the goals set for that student rather than comparing one student against another or comparing one student to the rest of the class can increase efficacy (Bandura, 1994).
- Help students establish specific, short-term goals that will challenge them, but goals that they view are attainable will increase efficacy (Schunk & Pajares, 2002).
- Cooperative learning structures, in which students work together and help one another, have the dual outcomes of improving self-efficacy and academic achievement (Bandura, 1994).
- When giving feedback on student performance, compare to past performances by the same student, don't make comparisons between students; this practice can increase efficacy for struggling students (Margolis & McCabe, 2006).

VIDEO DESCRIPTIONS

**Chapter 4: Strengthening Student Efficacy:
The Formative Assessment Process in Action**

Overview: The videos in this chapter illustrate the use of the EAA Classroom Protocol. The EAA Classroom Protocol has been developed to provide guidance to teacher learning teams and instructional leaders when implementing the formative assessment process into classroom culture.

All of the videos were recorded during the school day during instructional time.

Impact Teams use video often to scale up expertise regarding formative assessment with our Lesson Study and Micro-Teaching Protocols.

	Video 4-1: Self- and Peer Assessment: Writer's Workshop, Kindergarten – PS 45, District 31, NYC DOE	Jessica Vigliotti and Courtney McGinn, kindergarten ICT teachers at PS 45 in Staten Island, New York, are engaging their students in self-and peer assessment using the emergent writing continuum their kinder Impact Team developed. They recorded this video during instructional time.
	Video 4-2: Peer Assessment: Physical Education, First Grade, PS 9, District 31, NYC DOE	Deanna Marco, the principal of PS 9 in Staten Island, engaged these first graders in peer assessment during physical education. She recorded them in the hallway of the school, while the rest of the students were in PE. Jason Ericson, PE teacher at PS 9 developed the Bowling Peer Assessment Rubric.
	Video 4-3: Peer Assessment: Summary Writing, Fifth Grade, PS 5, District 31, NYC DOE	These 5th grade students are engaging in peer assessment for summary writing. Their teachers, Lana Regenbogen and Gabriella Pasquale, recorded the video in the hallway during class. They are ICT (Integrated Collaborative Teaching) teachers at PS 5 in Staten Island, NY.
	Video 4-4 Peer Assessment: Mathematics, Seventh Grade, IS 34, District 31, NYC DOE	These 7th grade students from Dayna Ugo's 7th grade math class, are engaged in peer assessment after a pre-test. Ms. Ugo had just co-constructed the success criteria for this assessment prior to this collaborative discussion. Ms. Ugo teaches at IS 34 in Staten Island, NY.

(Continued)

(Continued)

	Video 4-5 Scaffolding Peer Assessment: 9th Grade World History, LTHS, La Grange, IL	James Milkert, World History Teacher at Lyons Township High School (LTHS), is scaffolding peer assessment for his students. This video was recorded by the high school AV class.
	Video 4-6: Scaffolding Goal Setting: World History, Ninth Grade, LTHS, La Grange, IL	James Milkert, World History teacher at LTHS, is scaffolding goal setting with students after they engaged in peer assessment.
	Video 4-7 Modeling the Ladder of Feedback: American Studies, LTHS, La Grange, IL	Virgina Condon, an American Studies teacher at LTHS, is modeling using the Ladder of Feedback. Two high school students are demonstrating the feedback process for the class.
	Video 4-8: Feedback on Feedback: American Studies, High School, LTHS, La Grange, IL	Virgina Condon, an American Studies teacher at LTHS, engaging her students in peer assessment regarding literary analysis. Virgina is listening in and giving students feedback on their feedback to ensure quality and reliable peer assessment.
	Video 4-9: Feedback on Feedback: Chemistry, Eleventh Grade, LTHS, La Grange, IL	Michelle Harbin, a chemistry teacher at Lyons Township High School, is engaging students in peer assessment. Notice how she is giving students feedback on their peer feedback; this ensures quality peer assessment.

Equitable, Viable, and Coherent Curriculum   **5**

Creating Context for Efficacy

"The need for a cohesive and comprehensive curriculum that intentionally connects standards, instruction and assessment has never been greater than it is today."

Ainsworth, 2011

Mastery Moment: What strengths does your system have in creating a clear pathway for learning for students?

THE WHAT: EQUITY, VIABILITY, AND COHERENCE

Strengthening student efficacy requires systems to provide an *equitable, viable,* and *coherent* (EVC) curriculum. The curriculum provides a context for learning and is the first step to building a learning environment to strengthen efficacy. A quality learning environment and teaching methods can improve self-efficacy (Bandura, 1994). Quality curriculum doesn't just communicate the "what" to teachers; it also gives direction to the "how."

In addition, the curriculum must create time and space for students to participate in the formative assessment process since the five core formative assessment practices are grounded in strengthening efficacy beliefs for students. Our goal is for students to own their learning and master standards that are transferable across content areas and transferable to college and career. In addition, we want to empower the learners to be able to learn for themselves, give and receive feedback, set and monitor goals, and work collaboratively.

As educators work to address the challenge of having ALL students master state standards, one element has been identified as a key to successful school improvement efforts, that is, aligning what is tested to what is taught. With the advent of next generation standards, school districts across the country are striving to help teachers and administrators build the capacity to strengthen teaching and learning. Districts, schools, and regional centers are involving teachers from across the system to design and develop overarching K–12 curriculum that aligns the written, taught, and tested curricula. We have determined three factors that serve as lenses for designing or revising curriculum documents to keep students at the center of the learning and ensure fidelity of the formative assessment process:

1. equity

2. viability

3. coherence

Equity. An equitable curriculum has two dimensions. The first is *inclusion*, in other words ensuring that all students have access to *relevant* learning aligned to state standards. It seems obvious, but students need the opportunity to learn the content. Marzano (2003) has indicated that there is a discrepancy between the intended curriculum and the implemented curriculum. What is taught in the classroom does not necessarily align to the district's expectations. This discrepancy prohibits students from attaining the intended curriculum. Teachers must work collaboratively to unpack the curriculum so the team has a common understanding of the learning intentions. If the learning intentions are not communicated to students in a way that they understand, then they can't take ownership of the learning for peer and self-assessment. When teachers and students are clear and on the same page about the expectations, this can double the speed of learning (Hattie, 2009).

The second is *fairness*, which basically means making sure that personal and social circumstances—for example gender, socioeconomic status, or ethnic origin—should not be an obstacle to achieving educational potential (OECD, 2008). We subscribe to the notion that *fair isn't equal. Fair isn't equal* was introduced to the education community in 1988 by Allen Mendler and David Yellen. So what is a fair curriculum? Many define it as teaching everyone the same curriculum at the same time, adhering to a strict pacing guide, adhering to a textbook and using summative assessment to rank, sort, grade, and categorize students. It has been about what the teacher has been teaching, not what the kids are learning. We argue that doing so is the most unfair way to treat students. The focus needs to be on student learning rather than what the teacher is teaching.

Students are not the same. They have different motivations for their learning, different backgrounds, different needs, and different learning goals. An equitable curriculum acknowledges these differences and creates multiple opportunities for students to succeed. An equitable curriculum creates time and space for the formative assessment process to flourish. It creates ample time for students to peer and self-assess. It creates time for feedback aligned to success criteria. It creates time for revision and goal setting. It creates time for students to reflect on their learning and actually learn from their mistakes. An equitable curriculum puts ALL students at the center.

Viability. Time is a major consideration when determining the critical areas of focus in curriculum documents. A viable curriculum is attainable only with the benefit of time (Marzano, 2003). The content that teachers are expected to address must be adequately covered in the instructional time teachers have available. Unfortunately, there are too many standards to teach and learn in the typical school year. The state standards must be prioritized so students have time to learn and master essential skills and concepts.

We advocate prioritizing standards that are transferable across content areas and transferable to college and career. We call these standards *focus standards*. These standards will be the focus standards that teachers will assess using the formative assessment process with students. These standards will be delineated and communicated on curriculum maps so the system is on the same page. Rubrics and scoring guides will be developed for focus standards so students can monitor their own learning based on the success criteria. Teachers and students will also regularly monitor and celebrate student progress regarding mastering these essential standards: goal setting, student led conferences, exhibitions of learning, e-portfolios.

Coherence. Curriculum coherence is crucial in developing conceptual understanding of the big ideas in each course, grade level, and/or content area. A coherent curriculum builds ideas across time and disciplines by connecting ideas between relevant topics and by aligning instruction grounded in the formative assessment process. The term *coherent curriculum*, or aligned curriculum, refers to an academic program that is (1) well organized and purposefully designed to facilitate learning, (2) free of academic gaps and needless repetitions, and (3) aligned across lessons, courses, subject areas, and grade levels.

Learning intentions or targets are the foundation of a coherent curriculum. Big ideas are developed from focus standards and create relevance for the learning intentions. Having clear learning intentions is crucial to ensure intra- and inter-unit coherence. Intra-unit coherence results from developing integrated understanding by focusing on a few key big ideas rather than superficially covering many unrelated ideas in a single unit. Inter-unit coherence means that those same big ideas are addressed in multiple units within and across disciplines to construct integrated knowledge of those ideas across units and years.

Learning progressions or pathways must be developed from the focus standards and/or learning intentions for each unit to support inter- and intra-unit coherence. Learning progressions also represent the subgoals of the ultimate learning intention and/or standard. DeMeester & Jones (2009) suggest that learning progressions are presented to students as a continuum of learning, accounting for different rates of learning. The rate of individual students' progress may vary along the learning progressions, but progressions should ultimately connect the knowledge, concepts, and skills students develop as they evolve from novice to more expert performances (Heritage, 2008).

THE WHY: RESEARCH AND REASONS

Reason 1: Equity. *All* students must have the opportunity to learn the critical content of the curriculum (Marzano, 2012). However, there are too many students left out of the curriculum for a variety of reasons: mobility, lack of coherence, lack of clarity, or the dominance of a textbook-centered curriculum devoid of standards.

Reason 2: Efficacy: A quality learning environment and teaching methods can improve self-efficacy (Bandura, 1994). The following pedagogies can improve student self-efficacy:

- Cooperative learning structures, in which students work together and help one another, promote positive self-evaluations of capability and higher academic attainments (Bandura, 1994).
- Establish specific, short-term goals that will challenge the students, yet are still viewed as attainable (Pajares & Schunk, 2002).
- Help students lay out a specific learning strategy and have them verbalize their plan. As students proceed through the task, ask students to note their progress and verbalize the next steps (Pajares & Schunk, 2002).
- Compare student performance to the goals set for that student rather than comparing one student against another or comparing one student to the rest of the class (Bandura, 1994).

Reason 3: Clearly Defined Learning Progressions: Students are left out because the curriculum is not accessible to them. Students may not have the prerequisite skills and knowledge to be successful in mastering the grade-level standard(s). Learning progressions serve as entry points and pathways for students. Heritage, Kim, Vendlinski, and Herman (2009) explain that learning progressions are important to the development of progressive sophistication in skills within a domain.

Reason 4: Teacher Clarity. Teachers must clearly communicate the intentions of the lessons and the success criteria. Clear learning intentions describe the skills, knowledge, attitudes, and values that the student needs to learn. Teachers need to know the goals and success criteria of their lessons, know how students in their class are progressing, and know where to go next. Teacher clarity has a .75 effect size on student learning; this can almost double the speed of learning for students (Hattie, 2012).

Reason 5: Transferability. For students to be successful in college and career more emphasis must be placed on transfer of learning. Transfer of learning is the application of skills, knowledge, and/or attitudes that were learned in one situation to another learning situation (Perkins & Salomon 1992). Transfer of learning is a phenomenon of learning more quickly and developing a deeper understanding of the task if we bring some knowledge or skills from previous learning to a new learning situation. Therefore, to produce positive transfer of learning, we need to practice new learning in a variety of contexts.

THE HOW: 6 STEPS

Creating an equitable, viable, and coherent curriculum takes time and requires collaboration at all levels of the system. The following six steps can guide your team in the necessary actions to revise or develop curriculum that creates optimal conditions for learning.

Step 1: Determine Focus Standards

Identify and communicate the content considered essential for ALL students. This should be done in vertical Impact Teams at the elementary level for all subjects and in departmental Impact Teams at the secondary level. During this meeting, they should select focus standards to create coherence across the curriculum. This team meeting(s) should provide clear delineation of content that is essential versus that which is supporting. Teams may want to use the following lenses to choose focus standards:

- Are the perspective focus standards transferable across content areas?
- Are the standards transferable to college and career?

- Does existing data show a need for prioritizing perspective focus standards?
- Are the perspective focus standards a part of a crucial learning progression? How many years will students need to master this progression of learning?

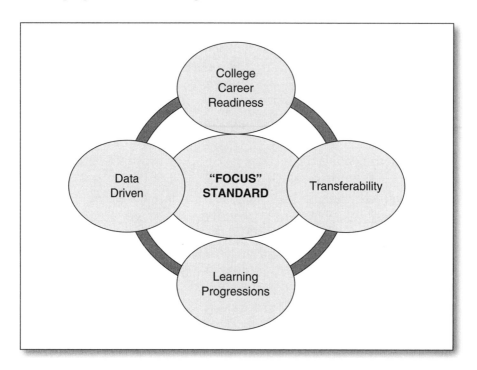

Step 2: Determine Time Needed

ALL students need the opportunity to learn the focus standards. During curriculum mapping the Impact Team should estimate the most amount of time needed for students to learn the focus standard and the amount of instructional time needed to teach them (English, 2010; Marzano, Kendall, & Gaddy, 1999). Obviously the amount of time to learn the focus standard(s) should not exceed the amount of instructional time available. Time needs to be dedicated to

- Teaching: explaining, modeling, guided practice, inquiry, feedback
- Learning: repeated practice, peer and self-assessment, feedback, revision, goal setting, reflection

Step 3: Unpack for Success

This protocol is designed for teams to get to know the standards. It ensures that the team is on the same page regarding learning outcomes as well as aligned in their approach to teaching the standard(s). Using this protocol gives teams the necessary understanding of the standards to partner with students in the formative assessment process. It engages teams in

- researching the standard,
- defining the key concepts and skills,
- defining cognitive rigor for task development,
- agreeing on relevance and big ideas/essential understandings,
- determining key competencies, and
- developing rubric-bound formative assessments.

Step 4: Organize and Sequence for Coherence

Organize and sequence the focus standards for coherence. Ensure that when the focus standards are placed in units of study that you consider the following:

- Focus standards that are more cognitively demanding should be introduced early on in the year to ensure that students have multiple opportunities to succeed. Hint: Depth of knowledge (DOK) is an excellent resource to determine time needed for mastery.
- The curriculum document signals to teachers that they must teach these standards explicitly toward the beginning of the year to have enough time for mastery of the standard.
- Focus standards should repeat across units so students have multiple opportunities to succeed.
- Supporting standards should be placed strategically to support focus standards.

Step 5: Celebrate Progress

Teachers and students monitor and celebrate student progress specific to mastering the focus standards

- Celebrations of learning are scheduled (student-led conferences, goal setting assemblies, exhibitions of learning, e-portfolios)
- Parents are invited

Step 6: Reengage for Equity

Fair isn't equal! Students are all different and don't learn at the same rate. We advocate for reengagement for students who need continued support. Students have all year to master the focus standards, and time must be allotted inside each subsequent unit and outside core instruction for reengagement and acceleration. Schools and districts have become quite innovative in finding extra time for reengagement. Some schools have designated time for reengagement for 30 minutes at the end of each day. Other schools have added 2 to 3 days after the unit summative assessment to their pacing calendar for time designated for reengagement. Some schools have created more practice opportunities inside their learning management system. Reengagement allows more time for students to be engaged in learning with a focus on the formative assessment process by

- Guiding students to set and monitor individual learning goals
- Allowing time for students to reflect on their learning
- Providing intervention and acceleration based on the focus learning progression(s)
- Utilizing small group instruction at the students' zone of proximal development
- Reassessing students after reengagement to determine impact

The implementation of the formative assessment process has inherent benefits for strengthening student efficacy. The diagram below outlines key pedagogies that strengthen efficacy.

DO	DON'T
• Ensure that students and teachers have a clear understanding of learning intentions and success criteria • Give multiple opportunities for students to succeed (mastery moments) • Guide students to set relevant short- and long-term goals • Create opportunities for students to collaborate regularly (safety) • Provide exemplars so students understand what success looks like (models of success) • Create regular opportunities for self- and peer assessment (feedback)	• Implement "lock-step" instruction that is inflexible and does not allow for student input. A formulaic type of instructional setting makes it harder for students to ask questions or become involved in the process (Bandura, 1994) • Implement teaching practices that compare students' performance against each other. This may raise the self-efficacy of the top students, but is likely to lower the self-efficacy of the rest of the class (Bandura, 1994) • Make what is taught more important than what is learned • Grade students when they are practicing

Purposeful Protocols

The following four protocols are utilized most often by Impact Teams to ensure implementation of an equitable, viable, and coherent curriculum. These four protocols support teachers in ensuring clarity for students:

- Unpacking for Success
- Calibration
- Lesson Study
- Microteaching

Unpacking for Success and Calibration are described in detail in this chapter.

UNPACKING FOR SUCCESS IN ACTION

This protocol is designed for teams to get to know the standards. It ensures that the team is on the same page regarding learning outcomes as well as aligned in their approach to teaching the standard(s). Using this protocol gives teams the necessary understanding to partner with students in the formative assessment process. It engages teams in

- researching the standard,
- defining the key concepts and skills,
- defining cognitive rigor for task development,
- agreeing on relevance and big ideas/essential understandings,
- determining key competencies, and
- developing rubric-bound formative assessments.

Unpacking should be done collaboratively and is used for ensuring alignment between what is taught and assessed. The key competencies developed in Step 6 are used to develop daily learning intentions and success criteria. The key competencies can also be used to develop success criteria for products and performances that align to the standard.

Step 1: Research the Standard: During this step the Impact Team can use open sources resources available to understand the standard at a deeper level. Each member from the team can research the standard using a different resource. Then they share what they learned with each other after researching. The notes can be put in Box 1.

Step 2: Determine the Skills & Concepts: During this step, the team categorizes the skills (verbs) and the concepts (nouns) in the boxes below.

Step 3: DOK and Rationale: The team determines the DOK range for the standard and briefly writes the rationale for the DOK.

Step 4: Learning Progression Notes: The team looks at the learning progression and takes notes regarding the learning progression since they may have students who read below grade level or above grade level. This helps the team understand what all students need to be successful.

Step 5: Relevance and Big Ideas: During this step, the team brainstorms how this standard is relevant in the real world and then develops possible big ideas for the standard. They also brainstorm a list of possible products and/or performance that would illustrate mastery of this standard.

Step 6: The team determines the key competencies for the standard. The team uses the key competencies to determine learning intentions and success criteria for products and performances relating to teaching the standard(s).

Unpacking for Success Example

Here is an example for Common Core State Standards (CCSS) RI.3.2. This third-grade team used the template to unpack the standard. It must be noted that the template is only a guide—and many teams have adapted the template to meet their learning needs.

(1) Research Standard(s): Copy the standard and use this box for your notes.

CCSS RI.3.2:

Determine the main idea of a text; recount the key details and explain how they support the main idea.

Notes:

- Students should be able to write a main idea sentence.
- They should be able to recount key details from the whole text, not just part of the text.

(2) Determine the Skills and Concepts	
Skills	**Concepts**
Determine	Main Idea
Recount	Key Details
Explain	Key Details (support the main ideas)

(3) DOK and Rationale

DOK 2:

- One clear main idea that is concrete. Text complexity would be the lower Lexile in the Lexile band.
- We could create multiple-choice items where they can choose the best main idea or key details.

DOK 3:

- The main idea for a DOK 3 item or task should be inferred.
- Multiple main ideas may exist in the text so there could be multiple correct answers.
- An extended response item with a rubric or checklist would be best to assess this standard and provide the best evidence for Impact Teams.

(4) Learning Progression (notes)

K–1: Students must name the topic and retell two to three key details from the book.

2: Students must name the topic and the focus of each paragraph or section (at least three paragraphs or three sections)

3: (This unpacking document)

4: Students must be able to write a summary

5: Students must be able to find multiple main ideas and support them with key details from the whole text.

(5) Relevance for Student	Big Ideas
<ul><li>Researchers</li><li>Cornell Notes</li><li>TV Reporters focus on the main ideas and the video footage gives you details.</li><li>Journalists focus on the main ideas.</li><li>When you write reports you have to communicate the main ideas and then support them with key details.</li></ul>	<ul><li>Good readers know that there are parts to whole relationships in text. The main ideas are the whole, and the key details are the parts that support the whole.</li><li>Good readers must determine importance in text. They have to know what is important and what is a detail.</li><li>Good readers summarize because it is an efficient way of communicating lots of information.</li></ul>

(6) Develop Key Competencies

- I can write a statement about the main idea.
- I can infer the main idea if it is not clearly stated in the text.
- I can write statements about at least three key details that support the main idea. Key details must come from the whole text.
- I can put the details in order as they appear in the text.
- I can write a brief explanation about how the key details support the main idea.
- I can use text features to help me figure out the main ideas and key details. (CCSS: RI.3.5)
- I can choose the best key details that support the main idea when given the main idea.
- I can write a main idea statement if I am given key details.

Team Reflection

How could you use the key competencies to develop rubrics, checklists, or plan your day-to-day learning intentions for instruction?

Note. There is a Math Unpacking example located in Appendix B. Notice how the team adapted the template and protocol to meet their needs.

From Key Competencies to Rubric

Example: This team used the key competencies from the Unpacking for Success protocol to create a *Main Idea Reading Rubric*. They developed this rubric to mirror the readers they had in their three- to four-combo class. Some readers were reading at the third-grade reading level (approaching on this rubric), some readers were reading at the fourth-grade reading level (meeting on this rubric), some readers were reading above grade level (exceeding on this rubric).

Progression	Approaching	Meeting	Exceeding
Lexile	450–790	770–980	770–980
F and P	N–P	Q–S	T–V
Key Ideas	• Can write a statement of the main idea.	• Can write a statement of the main idea. Main idea is usually inferred at this level.	• Can write a statement of each main idea (2). Main ideas are usually inferred at this reading level.
Details	• Can copy, paraphrase, or highlight 2 to 3 key details that support the main idea.	• Can copy, paraphrase or highlight 2 to 3 key details that support the main idea.	• Can paraphrase 2 to 3 key details that support main idea one. • Can paraphrase 2 to 3 key details that support main idea two.
Summary	• Can write a brief explanation about why the key details support the main idea.	• Can summarize the text. Summary must include the main idea of the text and the key details that support the main idea.	• Can summarize the text. Summary must include both main ideas of the text and the key details that support each main idea.

Note: See Appendix C for more examples of rubric-bound assessments.

Developing Learning Intentions

Example: This Impact Team used the Unpacking for Success protocol to create overarching learning intentions for day-to-day instruction based on the key competencies from the last step of the Unpacking for Success protocol.

- Today we are learning how to determine importance in text by writing a statement of the main idea.
- Today we are learning how to tell the difference between main ideas and key details.
- Today we are learning two different ways to find key details in a text that supports the articles main idea.
- Today we are learning how to determine what idea the author thinks is most important.
- Today we are learning how to determine the most important points in a text.
- Today we are learning that authors can have multiple main ideas and how to determine them when we read.
- Today we are learning how to summarize text by including the main ideas and key details that support them.

CALIBRATION IN ACTION

Purpose

To ensure that all members of the Impact Team are accurately scoring student work and that they are consistent in their scoring, creating inter-rater reliability. This protocol also ensures that the team's definition of *proficient* is the same.

Time

- 40 to 60 minutes
- This could also take extended periods of time depending on complexity of the student work

Resources

- Copies of the success criteria and/or rubrics

Materials

- Copies of unscored student work from different learning groups (single copies of up to eight different samples)
- Sticky notes
- Different colored pens and/or pencils

Step	Procedure	Time Allotment
EVIDENCE		
1	**Review the Evidence**	5 minutes
	• Team members review the rubrics and/or success criteria and the assignment.	
ANALYSIS		
2	**Independent Scoring**	5 minutes
	• Each team member scores one piece of student work without discussion. • Score is written on a sticky note on the back of the work.	
3	**Pass the Piece**	10–20 minutes
	• Team members pass the piece of student work on to a new member who then scores the work. • That score is then added to the back of the work. • Continue this process until each team member has scored each piece of work.	
4	**Discuss the Differences**	10 minutes
	• The team discusses the differences in the scores. • Each team members explains why they scored it the way they did, referencing the rubric and/or success criteria. • This continues until all pieces of student work have been discussed or until the team feels they are consistently applying the rubric/success criteria.	
ACTION		
5	**Revise the Rubric**	5–10 minutes
	• The team makes any needed changes to the rubric/success criteria to reflect the new understanding.	
6	**Clarify for Student Understanding**	5–10 minutes
	• The team discusses ways to ensure that all students understand and can use the rubric/success criteria for self- and peer assessment. • The team choose pieces of student work for examples of the success criteria and/or levels in the rubric.	

Team Reflection: How does your team collaboratively score student work to ensure inter-rater reliability when scoring student work aligned to rubrics?

NUTSHELL

An equitable, viable, and coherent curriculum creates the context for implementation of the formative assessment process. Three factors that serve as lenses for designing or revising curriculum documents to keep students at the center of the learning and ensure fidelity of the formative assessment process are:

1. equity

2. viability

3. coherence

Unpacking for success is a collaborative process that teacher teams use to ensure curricular clarity and consistency. The curriculum provides a context for learning and is the first step to building a learning environment to strengthen efficacy.

Read how Dr. Annette Villerot guided her team in creating an equitable, viable, and coherent curriculum in the Pflugerville Independent School District in Pflugerville, Texas. Quality curriculum creates optimal conditions for Impact Team implementation.

A developed written and viable curriculum is critical to the success of Impact Teams. There are several key components that ensure focused, targeted, and student-centered collaboration during Impact Team meetings: vertical articulation, focus/priority standards, unit guides that include big ideas and essential questions, unit based success criteria, formative assessments, and differentiated, tiered instructional strategies.

A major component and the foundation to the curriculum is a detailed vertical articulation using vertical learning progressions based on district focus standards. Within this learning progression, high stakes standards need to be identified through data. This helps determine which prerequisite skills and concepts in the learning progression may have led to lack of mastery. Focus standards are identified through four lenses: (1) data, (2) developmental need in learning progression, (3) transferability across content, and (4) skills for college and career readiness. The culmination of this information informs the identification of focus/priority standards, which determines the alignment of these standards in the scope and sequence. This scope and sequence blueprint is used to create units of study.

These units of study include the big ideas, essential questions, student success criteria, formative assessments, and differentiated instruction, which are all essential to successful Impact Teams. Teams discuss focus standards as an anchor to improved learning outcomes. When students struggle with a concept or skill, Impact Teams can refer to the learning progression to identify skills located earlier in the progression that need to be retaught for student success. Teams then determine success criteria for these skills. In other words, what do we as teachers need to convey to students so that they can recognize success during the upcoming lesson, and how do we differentiate instruction so that *all* students can *reach* that success criteria. Collaboration around these curricular components is the core to successful Impact Teams, because it creates a highly focused and targeted dialogue around tangible student outcomes.

In Pflugerville Independent School District, our goal is that our curriculum is developed with the new teacher in mind. With a comprehensive curriculum, our new teachers have the same opportunity to provide purposeful input and engage in planning with the most veteran of teachers. Our goal is for our curriculum to be designed so thoroughly that through the Impact Team collaborative process every teacher can provide every student with targeted instruction to meet his or her discreet needs.

CHECK-IN

Use the checklist below to assess your curriculum for equity, viability, and coherence. Determine next steps based on your results.

Action Steps	Not Yet	In Progress	Next Steps
Step 1: Determine Focus Standards			
Are the perspective focus standards transferable across content areas?			
Are the standards transferable to college and career?			
Does existing data show a need for prioritizing perspective focus standards?			
Are the perspective focus standards a part of a crucial learning progression? How many years will students need to master this progression of learning?			

Action Steps	Not Yet	In Progress	Next Steps
Step 2: Determine Time Needed			
Teaching: Explaining, Modeling, Guided Practice, Inquiry, Feedback			
Learning: repeated practice, peer and self-assessment, feedback, revision, goal setting, reflection, learning from mistakes			
Step 3: Unpack for Success			
Research the standard.			
Determine the learning progression.			
Determine the big ideas and essential questions.			
Determine relevant products or performances that would illustrate mastery of the focus standard(s).			
Determine possible student-friendly learning intentions based on the key competencies.			
Determine success criteria for relevant products, performances and/or strategies aligned to standards-based learning intentions.			
Step 4: Organize and Sequence for Coherence			
Focus standards that are more cognitively demanding should be introduced early on in the year to ensure that students have multiple opportunities to succeed. Hint: DOK is an excellent resource to determine time needed for mastery.			
The curriculum document signals to teachers that they must teach these standards explicitly toward the beginning of the year to have enough time for mastery of the standard.			
Focus standards should repeat across units so students have multiple opportunities to succeed.			
Supporting standards should be placed strategically to support focus standards.			

(Continued)

(Continued)

Action Steps	Not Yet	In Progress	Next Steps
Step 5: Celebrate Progress			
Celebrations of learning are scheduled (student-led conferences, goal setting assemblies, exhibitions of learning, e-portfolios).			
Invite parents to celebration.			
Step 6: Reengage for Equity			
Students monitor individual learning goals.			
Instructional time and extra practice are provided during core instruction to reengage; this time must be built into the pacing of the units of study.			
Some students need time outside of core instruction for intervention and acceleration based on the learning progression of the focus standard (this typically requires small group instruction).			
Students are reassessed after reengagement to understand impact.			

Collective Action:

1. Based on your curriculum assessment, what are your strengths?

2. Based on your curriculum assessment, what are your next steps in revising your curriculum?

3. What is the timeline for the revision process?

4. What transferable skill will be the focus of your first Impact Team Cycle?

VIDEO DESCRIPTIONS

Chapter 5: Equitable, Viable, Coherent Curriculum

Overview: The videos in this chapter illustrate the power of the curriculum in creating classroom clarity.

	Video 5-1: Creating Classroom Clarity: Pflugerville Independent School District, Pflugerville, TX	Dr. Alex Torrez and Dr. Annette Villerot from the Pflugerville Independent School District in Pflugerville, TX, discuss the importance of developing an Equitable, Viable, and Coherent curriculum in supporting classroom clarity.
	Video 5-2: Creating Classroom Clarity: PS 9, District 31, NYC DOE	Deanna Marco, principal of PS 9, discusses the importance of developing an Equitable, Viable, and Coherent curriculum in supporting classroom clarity.

Evidence to Inform and Act   **6**

"Learning from evidence requires a deeply personal appreciation of how it is essential to one's professional learning and growth. Without such appreciation and the associated skills, data use becomes an exercise in evaluating other people rather than in collective learning and improvement."

Robinson, 2011

Mastery Moment: Think of a time that your team was successful in using evidence to make decisions about strategic and responsive teaching. Describe a time when students used evidence to set learning goals and next learning steps.

THE WHAT: QUALITY EVIDENCE

What's the first word you think of when you hear the word *assessment?* We have asked this question to thousands of educators over the years and the overwhelming response is "Test!" We respectfully ask that you consider replacing the word *assessment* for *evidence* when doing Impact Team work. Why? Because in our world of student-centered learning, evidence is *more* than data and way *more* than test scores. Evidence is authentic, relevant, and valid information about student learning.

Teams always use evidence as the critical foundation for dialogue around learning. Evidence is always predetermined by the team based on the specific learning intention. Quality evidence is criteria based. Evidence is based on the competencies of learning, the markers of progress, the performance that demonstrates where the learner is in the learning progression. Evidence is what the teacher and learner are looking for to indicate where they are in the learning and what are the next steps in learning.

Quality evidence of learning can be:

- Samples of student work (criteria based)
- e-portfolio—a collection of student work over time
- student learning goals (student voice / student perception data)
- self- and peer assessment (feedback)
- self-reflection (student voice and/or student perception)
- Observation notes (from evidence walks/instructional rounds)
- Video
- Nonverbal communication from students (engagement or disengagement)

Quality evidence provides feedback to the team and/or learner and provides the basis for learning focused dialogue. Our point here is that evidence is

- specific to what is being learned,
- agreed upon in advance,
- visible,
- authentic,
- used to focus the conversations,
- the foundation of the analysis, and
- the springboard to action.

Without quality evidence, the teaming is just another forum for personal opinions. With quality evidence, the dialogue leads to analysis, and the analysis leads to collective action.

Evidence and Purposeful Protocols

All eight purposeful protocols use quality evidence to inform decisions and understand impact. In this chapter, we describe three protocols that use evidence to enhance collaborative inquiry:

1. The EAA Team Meeting (Analysis of Criteria-Based Evidence)

2. The Check-In and Case Study

3. Evidence Walks

THE WHY: RESEARCH AND REASONS

Quality evidence informs the team about what is happening right now in the learning. It prompts reflection, stimulates dialogue and debate, and fosters critical thinking around what, why, and how students are learning.

Reason 1: Improves the quality of teaching: For students to learn, they have to have access to the curriculum (see Chapter 5). And for them to access the curriculum, teachers need to know where they are in the learning progressions. Hence, teachers need to gather *evidence* to understand what students know and can do. With that *evidence* teachers can then design lessons for all students. According to Hattie (2009) a key "signpost" of excellence in education is when teachers engage in "*critical reflection in light of evidence about their teaching*" (emphasis added).

Reason 2: Improves student learning: We all learn by linking new ideas to what we already know. Discovering what we know is the process of gathering *evidence* through feedback from the teacher, from peers, and from self. Note that discovering this evidence is not just for the teacher but most important, for the student. For example, creating a portfolio of learning based on the success criteria and/or key competencies is *evidence* of progress and indicators of learning strengths. Receiving feedback from the teacher and/or peers based on success criteria is *evidence*, which leads to analysis and in turn, accelerates learning (Black & Wiliam, 1998).

Reason 3: Is a springboard to collective action: Analyzing quality evidence is important professional dialogue but is only an intellectual exercise unless it is followed by action. The action, however, needs to be based on specific quality evidence to ensure an appropriate instructional response. If the evidence is not current (old) or too general (not specific to the learning goal and/or rubric), then the instructional decisions have little chance of being effective. Are you making instructional decisions based on last year's test scores? Benchmark assessments from 3 months ago? Evidence is like feedback—it needs to be timely, relevant, and specific!

THE HOW: FOUR PURPOSEFUL PROTOCOLS

The following protocols are used most frequently to analyze and calibrate evidence during Impact Team meetings. Some protocols have been introduced in prior chapters.

- **EAA Team Meeting:** This protocol is used to analyze student work aligned to the focus standards. The protocol can also be used to analyze "student voice" data: goal setting, student reflections, and so on. The team determines criteria-based *evidence*, *analyzes* evidence, and takes collective *action* (EAA).

- **Check-In and Case Study:** This protocol is used to *check-in* on *actions* the team developed when they analyzed student work. Many times Impact Teams use this time to check-in with specific demographic groups to ensure all student needs are being met.

- **Evidence Walks:** Evidence walks are a form of instructional rounds (much like medical rounds) that help teachers and leaders look closely at a specific and predetermined practice central to the formative assessment process in a purposeful way. In small groups, teachers and leaders observe a colleague's classroom (volunteer) looking for evidence related to the practice. After the observation, the team provides *nonjudgmental* feedback based on specific criteria used as a lens for the evidence walk and determines next steps.

- **Calibration:** This protocol is designed to ensure that all members of the team are accurately scoring student work and that they are consistent in their scoring. Using student work samples from different levels, teachers anchor their understanding of progress through the calibration process. This protocol is described in Chapter 3 and 4 and the complete protocol and template is in Appendix A.

EAA TEAM MEETING PROTOCOL

Purpose

Impact Team meetings are rigorous, highly efficient, and result in evidence-based decision making. This protocol is used to analyze evidence based on the formative assessment process (student work, goal setting templates, reflections). The three-step process, **E**vidence • **A**nalysis • **A**ction, is followed for the meeting to:

- stay focused
- stimulate collaborative inquiry
- build knowledge
- share knowledge
- result in collective action

Time

- 40–60 minutes

Resources

- Access to shared team folder—unpacked standard, success criteria, learning progressions, team meeting notes template
- Projection (if possible)

Materials

- Student work by learning group, including students' self-assessment, and success criteria for the learning intention

Step	Procedure	Time Allotment
1	**EVIDENCE: Team members prepare evidence based on the following previously agreed-upon criteria**	5 minutes
	• Evidence is based on the success criteria of assessment product or performance aligned to the focus standard. • Evidence provides a window into students' thinking. • Evidence is disaggregated into 3 to 4 performance levels (exemplary, proficient, progressing, not yet). • Evidence is prepared for discussion prior to Impact Team meeting • Evidence includes diverse .data (formative assessment, self- and peer assessment, goal setting sheets, etc.).	
2	**ANALYSIS: Team members engage in collaborative inquiry based on the evidence.**	5 minute per level (15–20 minutes total)
	• Analysis is based on success criteria. • Analysis is by each performance level. • Strengths and next learning steps are based on root cause or *why*. • Next learning steps are determined for each performance level. • Next learning steps must reflect the learning progression.	
3	**ACTION: Team members collaboratively determine strategic action for each performance level based on the evidence and analysis**	5 minutes per level (15–20 minutes total)
	• Team creates instructional plan using clusters of high impact strategies for each performance level. • Team creates SMARTER goals for each performance level (Barber, 2011). • Team implements and monitors action plan for all learners. • Team reflects on instructional plan to determine impact on learning. • Team records collective actions that have the greatest impact.	

See an example of an Impact Team using the EAA Team Meeting Protocol and the Impact Team Meeting Peer Facilitation Scaffold in Appendix D.

Observe an Impact Team using the EAA Team Meeting Protocol to analyze student work to understand impact and take collective action.

CHECK-IN AND CASE STUDY

Purpose

During the learning cycle, Impact Teams check in with each other frequently to share successes and challenges based on their collective action agreements, after the team uses the EAA Team Meeting protocol to analyze student work. Rather than waiting until the end of the unit, they share artifacts, experiences, and student input and make timely corrections as needed. One successful practice we use is having each teacher choose students who are representative of a learning group and/or demographic group (e.g., long-term ELL student, at-risk student, gifted and talented student, etc.). They use these students' work as representative samples (case study) to make generalizations about teaching effectiveness. They study the same students throughout the school year:

- To monitor student progress
- To share successful strategies
- To share challenges
- To make midcourse corrections to ensure student progress
- To make generalizations about student sub-groups

Time

- 20–30 minutes

Materials

- Student and teacher artifacts

See an example of an Impact Team using the Check-In and Case Study Protocol in Appendix D.

Step	Procedure	Time Allotment
1	**Evidence**	5–10 minutes
	• Evidence: Team identifies evidence or samples of student work based on representative learning groups based on the EAA Team Meeting Protocol.	
2	**Analysis**	5–10 minutes
	• Analysis: Team analyzes evidence based on strengths/obstacles for each sample based on each student group.	
3	**Action**	5-10 minutes
	• Action: Team takes collective action by making mid-course corrections if necessary. Team archives effective practice for future.	

EVIDENCE WALK

Purpose

To develop a shared understanding of what high-quality instruction looks like specific to the formative assessment process. This protocol can be used to scale up expertise around the formative assessment five core practices districtwide or for a school site. To build a culture of relational trust, instructional leadership teams are invited to participate in the evidence walk.

Time

- Half Day (3–5 classes—host chooses the classes to visit and the focus)

Resources

- EAA Classroom Protocol

Materials

- Smart phones for video, photographs, and audio
- Note Taking
- Time Keeper

Step	Procedure	Time Allotment
1	**Setting the Stage**	5 minutes
	• Team members review the EAA classroom protocol. • Discuss the following question full group: What does it look like to learn, implement, and model the core practices of the formative assessment process?.	
2	**Focus of Learning**	5 minutes
	• How do students know what they are learning, why they are learning it, and what success looks like? • Briefly discuss what you would hope to hear and see regarding this focus.	
3	**Overview of Lessons and Context**	10–15 minutes
	• Host shares details regarding class contexts (class size, relevant student information). • Host shares the learning intentions and success criteria each teacher or school site is focusing on. • Host shares strategies specific to the EAA classroom protocol (the formative assessment process). • Host shares what questions they are curious about specific to the formative assessment process (e.g., We have been wondering about this . . . . We have been trying this . . . . We want to know what you think about this . . . .). • Group defines what questions they will ask to students when entering the classroom (e.g., What are you learning? How do you know you will be successful? Why are you learning this?).	
4	**Review Norms for Observation**	5 minutes
	• Observations recorded in writing, photos, audio, and so on • Evidence is based on what participants see and hear. • Descriptive and nonjudgmental.	
EVIDENCE		
5	**Observations**	10–15 minutes (each class; this can vary)
	• Define task observed. • Describe what students are saying and doing. • Describe what teacher is saying or doing. • Environmental Scaffolds.	

ANALYSIS		
6	**Observation Analysis (Debrief)**	5–10 minutes
	• Sharing of observations (jig saw). • What were the students able to do? What are their strengths? • Analyze the picture this evidence presents.	
ACTION		
7	**Responding to Host**	5–10 minutes
	• Respond to host's questions. • Determine next steps for professional learning. • Discuss any questions raised. • Set goals for the individual and/or group.	

Team Reflection: Describe how your team or school ensures fidelity to the Formative Assessment 5 Core Practices. How does your team use student voice as a data point?

NUTSHELL

Evidence is specific information about learning and is key to making informed collaborative decisions. Too often teams base decisions on perspective, opinion, or outdated data. Our intention is to present a broader concept of evidence to stimulate team dialogue around relevant information that informs both teachers and students about what is happening in the learning process.

CHECK-IN

With your team, use the rubric on p. 102 to reflect on what and how you use evidence to inform teaching and learning. During your reflection, add ideas and next steps to enhance your collaborative practices.

Foundational Components	Not Yet	Sometimes	Always
Sources of evidence			
Team determines evidence sources in advance of the learning (must be criteria based).			
Evidence is specific, timely, and calibrated.			
Team uses multiple sources of student evidence: formative/student work, student perception, performance, self-regulation, and so on as a basis for collaborative inquiry.			
Team uses multiple sources of teaching evidence: video, evidence walks, student work, lesson study, and so on as a basis for collaborative inquiry.			
What's next?			
Process: EAA			
Team uses purposeful protocols to create and calibrate evidence (EAA Team Meeting, Calibration, Check-In and Case Study, Evidence Walks).			
Evidence is used to discover instructional insights to meet the needs of all learners.			
What's next?			

VIDEO DESCRIPTIONS

Chapter 6: Evidence to Inform and Act

Overview: The videos in this chapter illustrate our thought partners using Impact Team Protocols to guide Impact Team Inquiry Cycles.

	Video 6-1: Model — EAA Team Meeting Protocol in Action: Analyzing Student Work — LTHS, La Grange, IL	This video shows Dr. Paul Bloomberg modeling peer facilitation of the EAA Team Meeting Protocol – analyzing student work for the World History Team at LTHS.
	Video 6-2: Gradual Release — EAA Team Meeting Protocol in Action: Analyzing Student Work – LTHS, La Grange, IL	This video shows Jamie Bronuskas, Chemistry Peer Facilitator at LTHS, facilitating the EAA Team Meeting protocol with her Chemistry team. Dr. Paul Bloomberg is coaching her using the EAA Team Meeting implementation rubric.

Leading Model Teams

7

"Principals can no longer lead instructional reform alone: The voice and expertise of teachers are essential to improve teaching and learning."

Wilhelm, 2013

Mastery Moment: Describe the best leadership experience you've had. What conditions were present to make this experience memorable?

THE WHAT: LEADING FOR CHANGE

Contrary to common belief, school leadership is not just one person, not just the principal. Rather, it is a collective commitment by the adults in the school to make a difference in the lives of all students. Fullan (2010) argues that truly effective educational leadership creates working conditions in which professional growth, commitment, engagement, and "constant spawning of leadership in others" are fostered. It is leadership that develops collective capacity and builds student and teacher efficacy.

When it comes to leading, school change is created through the collective, by people interacting, trying things out, testing the waters, improving their practice, reflecting on their impact, adjusting to better practice, and sharing their learning. We call this *collective leadership*.

Any educator who has been in the profession for more than a few years knows that all-school change takes time, perseverance, and unrelenting commitment. As Ringo Starr sang, *"It don't come easy, ya know, it don't come easy."* After working together with schools in their change efforts and carefully observing those who make progress and those who do not, so much, we have developed a change strategy for implementation of the Impact Team Model that has had remarkable results. It's called the Model Teams Approach (MTA). This change model is based on the gradual release model that builds capacity from within through coaching, practice, and feedback. This process accesses the four sources of efficacy and builds collective efficacy.

The MTA is based on the common sense notion of working with what you've got—strategic resourcing (time and people), working out the kinks before all-school implementation. The Model Team becomes the unit of change and a resource for other teams in the change process. This avoids the pitfalls of all-system change:

- Not enough time to learn and practice gradually
- Not enough coaching to improve the practice
- Not enough expertise to use the protocols effectively
- Lack understanding of the research or value of the practice
- Lack of opportunity to differentiate the process to meet the needs of each team
- Lack of administrative support since they are trying to implement full system

In our experience, when systems try to implement this model with everyone, they are not able to leverage the four sources of efficacy. Whether the initiative is worthy or not, it now has a bad rap in the school and *this too has passed.*

By starting small, with one or two teams, and developing leadership and facilitation skills in the process, abundant support is provided, missteps are welcomed, feedback flows, and collaborative practices are enhanced. The MTA is built around the four sources of efficacy.

The Goal is Efficacy—Teacher, Student, and Team

Leading Impact Teams is about leading for efficacy, designing a system, and building structures and processes that strengthen the four sources of efficacy:

1. Mastery moments

2. Models of success

3. Feedback

4. Safety

The MTA is based on the old-school wisdom of *start small to go far* and requires three ingredients:

1. Collective leadership: The principal and the leadership team's active involvement in promoting and participating in the learning process

2. A team (or two) willing to learn—to try it on for size

3. A belief in the power of the formative assessment process to strengthen student efficacy

Using the MTA, in 4 to 6 months school leadership has developed the expertise to build capacity across the system. They have learned to

- Facilitate an effective team meeting;
- Use protocols to guide collaborative inquiry;
- Determine quality evidence to understand impact;
- Analyze quality evidence; and
- Agree upon collective actions that have high impact.

These Model Teams also serve as a viable resource to move the practice out to other teams in the school. In fact, some of our clients have termed this practice Adopt-a-Team.

Going back to the *it don't come easy* notion, the MTA makes all-school change doable from within and sustained high-impact collaboration an embedded school practice.

THE WHY: RESEARCH AND REASONS

There is a strong causal relationship between instructional leadership, teacher collaboration, teacher efficacy beliefs, and student achievement (Goddard, Goddard, Kim, & Miller, 2015). Collective leadership is an intersection of all four components and is a systemic process that ensures school-wide progress.

Reason 1: Contributes to building collective efficacy. Collaboratively learning and leading builds the belief that together they have the expertise to do great things. When teachers share responsibility for leading, they feel empowered. When they feel empowered, they feel confident that they can make a difference. When they believe they can make a difference, they do! These lead to mastery experiences that not only build collective efficacy but also serve as models of success for others (Eells, 2011).

Reason 2: Improves the quality of learning. Engaging all teachers in relentlessly and collaboratively focusing on improving student learning reaps great rewards (Fullan & Quinn, 2016). Changing the paradigm from accountability (test scores) to ensuring all students are making *progress* empowers teachers to be responsive to student learning, to be a key part of the collective to make a difference. "The more willing principals are to spread leadership around, the better for the students" (Harvey & Holland, 2012).

Reason 3: Improves the quality of teaching. Learning together, taking action together, analyzing the impact of those actions, and responding strategically improves instruction. The quality of teacher collaboration positively influences the quality of teaching and student achievement (Ronfeldt, Farmer, McQueen, & Grissom, 2015). Accepting their role as key contributors to and leaders for student success, teachers engage in identifying problems of practice, successes, and challenges. They are continuously engaged in a learning cycle, developing effective practices that result in increased student achievement.

Reason 4: Builds and sustains collective commitment. Sharing a common purpose within a collaborative culture leads to ongoing experiences that present challenges, successes, dilemmas, and frustrations, but ultimately result in improved learning for all students. Operating from a strength-based mindset and committed to collaboratively learning, teachers become leaders, leaders are learners, and change in practice evolves. These mastery experiences interspersed with challenges and failures strengthen the resolve of the collective to make a difference for all students, the bedrock belief of the school.

School improvement is simply not a one-man band. "In fact, if test scores are any indication, the more willing principals are to spread leadership around, the better for students . . . . Principals may be relieved to find out, moreover, that their authority does not wane as others' waxes. Clearly school leadership is not a zero-sum game" (Harvey & Holland, 2012).

THE HOW: THE MODEL TEAMS APPROACH

1. Lead from within—commitment of the principal and leadership team

2. Invite a team(s) to learn and model effective collaboration

3. Redefine formative assessment

The MTA is an implementation model that operationalizes the four sources of efficacy by building expertise through practice that results in mastery experiences for teams. These teams then become models for other teams.

If we have learned anything from the past two decades of school reform, it is that trying to do all-school change in one fatal swoop is risky business. Trying to implement change takes tremendous resources regarding time and people, and schools rarely have access to enough resources to ensure fidelity of practice for the entire school. Then when things go awry and the practice does not result in the advertised outcomes, teachers become disenchanted and back away from the desired change. "This too shall pass," and it does, leaving a bad taste from whatever the initiative was.

To prevent this negative experience, we follow Viviane Robinson's (2011) advice and use "strategic resourcing" to ensure the new practice results in success. That is, we deal in reality and wisely use what resources are available to support the change.

We begin with the principal and the leadership team (John Kotter [1996] calls this the "guiding coalition") who have committed to learn and practice the Impact Team Model. They start by doing the Impact Team pre-assessment (see Appendix F) to see where their school is in

- understanding and implementing the formative assessment process, and
- understanding and practicing effective teaming.

The principal and leadership team then use the Evidence • Analysis • Action (EAA) meeting protocol to analyze the pre-assessment and to determine next steps. Typically the leadership team begins with engaging interested teachers and teams in going deeper into student-centered learning around the formative assessment process. There are 4 steps to the Model Team Approach:

1. Lead from within

2. Invitation to team

3. Redefine formative assessment

4. Execution as learning

(1) Lead From Within

We've known for years that school improvement takes all hands on deck. Barth (2013) posits that a school should be a community of leaders—not just a principal and a lot of followers. Witness the past decade of school reform where principals were replaced to improve the school yet rarely did that process result in improving student performance.

A school's greatest resource for improvement is its teachers. Under the roof of every school is a wealth of expertise. The challenge is to create ways for teachers to reveal themselves as innovators, experts, champions of student learning, and passionate professionals.

The Principal

The principal is the critical driver in the wheelhouse of the MTA. Without the principal's unwavering commitment to develop capacity and improve practice through the Impact Team Model, there may be pockets of teachers and some teams who will embrace and practice the process, but there will never be all-school change.

The principal's role is clearly defined. She or he must understand what it is to build a culture of efficacy, why it is key to student-centered learning, and how to go about creating the conditions to build student, teacher, and collective efficacy. With that commitment comes a call to action. That action is a commitment and concomitant actions to lead the Model Team, that is, to walk the talk.

> *The most powerful way that school leaders can make a difference to the learning of their students is by promoting and participating in the professional learning and development of their teachers.* (Robinson, 2011)

Peer Facilitator

Trained peer facilitators guide their teammates through inquiry, investigation, and collaborative learning. The peer facilitators are provided additional training in the eight purposeful protocols and are models for investigative practice, risk taking, and knowledge sharing. They are uniquely positioned to both guide the team as well as learn with the team. As members of the Impact Team, they walk in the same shoes—trying out the lessons, partnering with the students, and focusing on understanding their impact.

Impact Teams choose a teammate who is interested in learning facilitation skills and guiding the process. The peer facilitator is responsible for ensuring the team operates with efficiency and effectiveness. The role of the facilitator is to

- establish roles and norms;
- facilitate the meeting—adhering to time frames, topics, and outcomes;

- prompt robust dialogue and discourse through appreciative inquiry; and
- stimulate new learning.

Peer-facilitators are uniquely positioned to model "a leap of faith," frame the work as an investigation, help the group "stick with it," and guide protocol use as a full participant in the inquiry process. Teacher-facilitators are trying out in their classrooms the same lessons as everyone else in the group. (Gallimore, Emerling, Saunders, & Goldenberg, 2009)

See Appendix D-3 for peer facilitator question stems to guide teachers through the analysis of student work for the EAA Team Meeting Protocol (analysis of student work).

The Instructional Leadership Team (ILT)

Schools typically have in place a building leadership team representing the various grade levels, subject areas, and specialists in the school. We recommend using what already exists, with the caveat that all members are on board with the two key ingredients of collective leadership:

1. a commitment to building teaching expertise school-wide

2. activating change through effective teaming

If there are those who cannot commit, choose teachers who can and will. Perhaps the leadership team (guiding coalition) will be a subgroup of the Instructional Leadership Team (ILT). Even two or three representative teacher leaders are enough initially to implement the MTA. These teachers are not a part of the model team itself; rather, they are teacher leaders interested in learning the process to share with their cohort later, down the road.

(2) Invitation to Become a Model Team

Through the pre-assessment (see Appendix F), the principal and leadership team identify one or two teams that might be interested in improving their collaborative practice and invite them to join in learning the MTA. Find a team that can be successful and become shepherds of the work. The commitment is to use their existing team time to learn the Impact Teams' process. With this commitment and the formative assessment background (above), they're ready to go.

(3) Redefining Formative Assessment

Based on the evidence from the Impact Team pre-assessment (see Appendix F) the principal, leadership team, and model team cocreate a plan to address the learning needs of the team around the formative assessment process (see Chapter 4).

Focusing on an upcoming unit, the team unpacks the standard (see Chapter 5) to create a rubric-bound assessment. The team begins the process of learning how to partner with students. At this point, they are learning how to:

- Prioritize standards for a unit of study
- Collaboratively understand the expectations of the focus standard(s)
- Create rubric-bound assessments based on the key competencies
- Engage students in the formative assessment process
- Calibrate their evaluation of student work

(4) Execution as Learning

The MTA uses the gradual release of responsibility model (Duke & Pearson, 2002).

Gradual Release

Essentially, modeling, practice, and feedback are the way the MTA works. This is an execution-as-learning process in which teams learn protocols as needed through coaching and modeling. This implementation process is authentic, organic, and develops a variety of skills and knowledge in context, such as how to:

- Facilitate a meeting
- Enhance the formative assessment process in the class
- Use protocols for specific purposes
- Determine and use quality evidence
- Do critical analysis to the root cause of student learning
- Determine the highest impact strategies to address root cause
- Understand impact

In the MTA, the Impact Team consultant works directly with the model team, the principal, and the peer facilitator, going through four short formative assessment cycles to learn and practice the Impact Team process. We typically focus on two protocols first:

1. EAA Team Meeting (Analyzing Student Work)—Appendix A-1

2. Check-In and Case Study—Appendix A-2

Over the course of four meetings the principal, peer facilitator, and team learn how to use protocols to understand their impact on student learning.

- **Time 1**: *Consultant facilitates* the Impact Team meeting using the team's first round of formative assessment data using the three-step Impact Team protocol EAA. After the meeting, the principal, peer facilitator, ILT, and consultant debrief the process based on the EAA team rubric.
- **Time 2**: *Consultant co-facilitates with the principal using the three-step Impact Team protocol EAA based on* the second round of formative assessment data. After the meeting, the principal, peer facilitator, ILT, and consultant debrief the process based on the EAA team rubric.
- **Time 3**: *The principal and peer facilitator facilitate* this Impact Team meeting using the third round of formative assessment data. Consultant, principal and ILT observe the peer facilitator and provide feedback based on the EAA team rubric.
- **Time 4**: *The peer facilitator facilitates* this Impact Team using the fourth round of formative assessment data. Consultant, peer facilitator, and ILT observe and give feedback based on the EAA team rubric.

At the end of this chapter, read a complete case study of how one large urban school implemented the Impact Team Model through the MTA. Also please see the companion site for video footage of the MTA in action.

Next Steps: Sharing the expertise

Now that your school has at least one team that is proficient at the Impact Team process and at least two facilitators who can guide the teams, what next? Since the Impact Team Model is all about identifying and leveraging the expertise in the building, many of our schools move to what we call the Adopt-a-Team model where the functional Impact Team models the process for other interested teams. Teams and leaders then have the opportunity to observe and practice with the Model Team(s) in a variety of ways:

- Using video of the Model Team, the peer facilitator and/or principal teaches and coaches other interested teams
- Using the fishbowl set up, teams observe the Model Team in action and debrief with the team using the Impact Team implementation rubric
- Members of the Model Team mentor other teams using the Impact team implementation rubric
- The trained peer facilitator takes on another team and coaches them to proficiency using the Model Team approach (release of responsibility over four meetings)

The point is you now have the resources to share the collaborative expertise. It is not a perfect process, it's a learning process. Some teams take to it quickly and are relieved and excited to finally experience efficient and focused meetings that result in actions that have impact. Other teams take a bit more time to practice. But as with all learning, practice with feedback moves the teams to a level of collaborative expertise that builds collective teacher efficacy school and system-wide.

NUTSHELL

Educators are professional learners. We like to learn, we know how to learn, and with the complexity of our profession, we need to constantly learn to meet the challenging needs of our students. However, putting our new learning into practice is where the rubber hits the road and where we encounter the challenges of implementation. Our MTA is designed to mitigate the support demands required in all-school change by starting with one or two teams and developing leadership and facilitation skills through the execution-as-learning process.

CHECK-IN

Use the checklist below to guide leadership in implementing the MTA. Determine next steps based on your results.

Action Steps	Not Yet	In Progress	Next Steps
(1) Lead From Within			
Principal commits to promoting and participating in the Model Team Approach.			
The Instructional Leadership Team (ILT) commits to activating change through effective teaming.			
Principal and ILT use the Impact Teams Pre-Assessment to determine learning strengths and next steps.			
(2) Invitation to Become a Model Team			
Based on pre-assessment, interested teams volunteer to learn the MTA.			
Framework for MTA is communicated to the team.			
Model Team coconstructs the cycle to ensure ownership.			
(3) Redefining Formative Assessment			
Based on pre-assessment, the Model Team unpacks focus standards for a unit of study.			
The Model Team develops rubric-bound assessments based on key competencies.			
(4) Model Teams in Action: Four Meetings			
Time 1: Consultant facilitates Meeting 1.			
Time 2: Consultant and principal co-facilitate Meeting 2.			
Time 3: Peer facilitator facilitates Meeting 3.			
Time 4: Peer facilitator facilitates Meeting 4.			
Video may be used to build capacity across the district.			

CASE STUDY

Katherine Smith, Coordinator of Testing and Research at Lyons Township High School, described how her school used the Model Team Approach to build capacity with the Impact Team Model. Read how this large comprehensive high school participated in this process.

Lyons Township High School District 204

In 1888, Lyons Township High School District 204 (LTHS) was founded in the suburbs of LaGrange and Western Springs, Illinois, 16 miles southwest of downtown Chicago. Spanning across two campuses, the one high school district presently educates over 4,000 high school students from the communities of Brookfield, Burr Ridge, Countryside, Hodgkins, LaGrange, LaGrange Highlands, LaGrange Park, McCook, Western Springs, and Willow Springs. Dedicated to affirming the school's century-old motto, Vita Plena, the quest for the fulfilling life, Lyons Township High School is proud to offer its students over 300 courses and opportunities including (but not limited to) 26 Advanced Placement courses, 9 dual credit courses, 6 language programs, an automotive program, Cisco Networking Certification, Deep Diving Certification, and pilot licensure.

> **4000+ Students**
>
> - 74% White
> - 18% Hispanic
> - 4% Black

The Context

During the 2009–2010 school year, the staff of Lyons Township High School established professional learning communities (PLCs) in an effort to ensure all students were learning more. Following the work of Rick and Rebecca DuFour, PLCs attempt to answer the questions:

1. What should all students know and be able to do?

2. How will we know when all students have learned?

3. What will we do when a student hasn't learned?

4. What will we do when a student has learned or reached proficiency?

However, when confronted with changing state standards and assessments, a deeply rooted system of course leveling, and a traditionally private teaching culture, collaboratively answering these questions proved to be problematic for LTHS's PLCs. The four PLC questions did not provide an efficient protocol or structure for scaling up collaborative inquiry across LTHS. In addition, it was important to the leadership at LTHS that we had a focus on developing assessment capable learners. We wanted our students to be independent learners, who could self-regulate.

> "My PLC has struggled with balancing the work load of what the district is asking us to do vs. what PLCs are actually supposed to do. With my time working with the Bloomberg team, I have realized that we should be analyzing student learning, discussing success criteria, looking at where our students struggle and why, and using this information to inform our instruction."
>
> —Bridget McGuire, Math Teacher

Curricular Work:
An Easy Place to Get Stuck

For 4 years, teams worked diligently identifying their course level Enduring Understandings/Big Ideas and content-based Essential Outcomes/Learning Intentions, and designing common summative assessments aligned to course-level Essential Outcomes. Biweekly PLC meetings were consumed with curricular work. As membership on the PLCs changed annually with new teaching schedules, curricular work was often repeated to incorporate the voice of new PLC members. While staff was making every effort to answer Questions 1 and 2 (as listed above), conversations were predominantly focused on teaching as opposed to student learning.

A New Plan

To effectively shift the conversation from teaching to learning, we needed to

- identify that with which all students must demonstrate proficiency, prior to completing a particular course (regardless of the level of the course);
- establish common formative assessments as opposed to summative assessments;
- conduct meaningful and focused conversations around student performance during the units of instruction;
- conclude PLC meetings with an instructional action plan to implement prior to the next team meeting; and
- facilitate structured follow-up conversations to determine where students were performing after the instructional action plans were implemented.

Getting Back on Track

Step 1: Identify the Common Denominator

To move forward, we identified the common denominator concerning student academic expectations. The Illinois State Standards (an adapted version of the Common Core State Standards [CCSS]) clearly articulate student English, math, and disciplinary literacy expectations at each grade level. Relying on state and national standards alleviates internal disputes and places the focus on the academic skills with which all students in a grade level are expected to demonstrate proficiency.

Step 2: Establish a Job-Embedded Professional Learning Plan with Articulated Outcomes

When developing a professional learning plan, LTHS consulted studies on adult learning. Studies conducted by Learning Forward (2011), Jim Knight and Jake Cornett (n.d.), and Doug Reeves (2010) concluded high quality professional learning is aligned to state standards and local goals, facilitated frequently in teams as part of an ongoing learning cycle, and involves goal-setting, action planning, and the application of research-based instructional strategies.

AUGUST 12, 13				All 10 Teams	
OCTOBER 20		**OCTOBER 21**		**OCTOBER 22**	
Periods 1 & 2	English II	Period 1	Geometry	Periods 1 & 2	World History
Periods 3 & 4/5	English III	Period 2 & 3	Health	Periods 3 & 4/5	U.S. History
Periods 7/8 & 9	Algebra	Period 4/5 & 6/7	Biology	Periods 7/8 & 9	Consumer Education
Period 10	Geometry	Period 9 & 10	Chemistry	Period 10	Planning Period with Administrators
JANUARY 20		**JANUARY 21**		**JANUARY 22**	
Periods 1 & 2	English III	Period 1	Health	Periods 1 & 2	U.S. History
Periods 3 & 4/5	Algebra	Period 2 & 3	Biology	Periods 3 & 4/5	Consumer Education

Periods 7/8 & 9	Geometry	Period 4/5 & 6/7	Chemistry	Periods 7/8 & 9	English II
Period 10	Health	Period 9 & 10	World History	Period 10	Planning Period with Administrators
MARCH 25		**MARCH 26**		**MARCH 27**	
Periods 1 & 2	Algebra	Period 1	Biology	Periods 1 & 2	Consumer Education
Periods 3 & 4/5	Geometry	Period 2 & 3	Chemistry	Periods 3 & 4/5	English II
Periods 7/8 & 9	Health	Period 4/5 & 6/7	World History	Periods 7/8 & 9	English III
Period 10	Biology	Period 9 & 10	U.S. History	Period 10	Planning Period with Administrators
MAY 11		**MAY 12**		**MAY 13**	
Periods 1 & 2	Geometry	Period 1	Chemistry	Periods 1 & 2	English II
Periods 3 & 4/5	Health	Period 2 & 3	World History	Periods 3 & 4/5	English III
Periods 7/8 & 9	Biology	Period 4/5 & 6/7	U.S. History	Periods 7/8 & 9	Algebra
Period 10	Chemistry	Period 9 & 10	Consumer Education	Period 10	Planning Period with Administrators
June 3, June 4		**All 10 Teams**			

As a result of the research, LTHS developed a professional learning plan that allowed 10 teams and an administrative team to meet with an external consultant six times throughout the course of the school year. While the work, during the first year, continued to be curricular, it was aligned to the CCSS, skill-based, formative, and common for all levels of the course.

By the end of the first year, all involved teams

- aligned their course curriculum (map) and Essential Outcomes/ Learning Intentions to the CCSS;
- developed common formative assessments concerning transferrable skills aligned to specific CCSS;

- developed a common summative assessment aligned to specific CCSS; and
- selected and implemented research-based instructional literacy strategies to use when teaching course Essential Outcomes and the literacy-based CCS.

Step 3: Target Teams and Invite Participants

2014–2015: Targeted Teams	
Department	Team
Language Arts	English II English III
Math	Algebra Geometry

To provide teams appropriate levels of support, LTHS had to focus the professional learning efforts on a limited number of teams. The 10 courses that establish foundational skills and impact the greatest number of students early on in their high school career were targeted to be the first teams that would receive support. A staff member from each level of the course (prep, accel, honors) was asked to participate on the team, as well as the special education cross-categorical teacher and a literacy team member. This structure allowed for a smaller-subset of the course teachers to set equitable expectations for students in the course.

Step 4: Locate the Right Help

The work that LTHS needed to do involved literacy, common core alignment, and assessment development and would eventually involve team structure and dynamics. To find a well-rounded consultant, we contacted Corwin and were put in touch with Dr. Paul Bloomberg. To ensure Dr. Bloomberg had the appropriate expertise and an ability to establish and expand relational trust personality across our school, we invited him to facilitate a workshop before signing a year-long contract. It was important to LTHS that we found a consultant who could maintain a focus on the formative assessment process, which we had begun to study in 2012. We wanted to continue this process through the lens of CCSS implementation because of its impact on student learning.

Step 5: Ask for Feedback and Invite Continued Participation

After 1 year of work with Dr. Bloomberg, all 10 teams achieved the curricular outcomes. These curricular outcomes had to be met before the conversation could shift to what students were learning. Before embarking on a second year of targeted professional learning, all 10 teams were consulted about the next steps and all team members were asked to continue. For LTHS, 96% of the staff volunteered to continue. The two staff members opting not to continue were replaced with two of their coworkers.

IMPACT Teams: A Simple Structure to Refocus PLCs

To develop assessment capable learners, paradigm shift had to occur at LTHS; we had to refocus our existing PLC structure. Educators had to abandon their traditional teacher talk concerning what they were teaching and had to begin to discuss what was being learned and how it was being learned by their students. The leadership at LTHS desired traditionally private teachers to publically share their craft and meaningfully discuss their students' performance; they had to be provided continual support and be provided an efficient structure to learn together resulting in the development of professional capital. LTHS discovered this support and structure in the IMPACT Team Model.

IMPACT Teams are teams of educators that collaborate on behalf of students. For LTHS, the 10 targeted teams that worked with Dr. Bloomberg in 2014–2015 to develop rigorous formative assessments aligned to the Common Core transitioned to IMPACT Teams in 2015–2016. Together, the educators on these teams are building their professional capacity by scaling up their expertise. Through the use of seven protocols, they are operationalizing the formative practices that yield the highest rates of learning.

LTHS's 10 teams are currently focusing on implementing the EAA protocol with fidelity. This is a three-phase protocol that has provided a framework to our teams to have a meaningful discussion centered on student learning demonstrated through a formative task. The protocol begins with team members sorting student work into the quality levels identified by the rubric, which is associated with their performance task. For each level of work, the team

- examines the evidence by asking: What success criteria were the students able to achieve? What criteria do they still need to demonstrate to achieve the next level of proficiency?;
- analyzes the evidence by determining what skills and abilities allowed the students to demonstrate proficiency, and what skills and proficiencies potentially prohibited the students from reaching the next quality level; and
- creates an action plan (relevant to the needs of each quality level) to implement by their next meeting.

"This Evidence • Analysis • Action Protocol gives us a process to look at student work, analyze and take action on how we will go about helping our students achieve the skill or target of our focus. So often our PLCs are given a directive for what to accomplish and the ultimate goal has always been to get to analyzing student work but the HOW we do that has been missing. The Evidence • Analysis • Action Protocol provides that plan and structure so that real progress and teaching can take place."

—Virginia Condon,
English Teacher

When implementing this protocol, team members leave their meeting with a plan that is instructionally differentiated. The next time they meet, they engage in the Check-In Protocol to ensure student growth is being achieved or they engage in the Microteaching Protocol as a means of learning an instructional practice focused on the formative assessment process and implemented by one of their team members.

Building Capacity: The Model Teams Approach

At LTHS, we wanted IMPACT Teams to consistently focus conversations on student learning. To guarantee this end, our team members are participating in a gradual release model (The Model Teams Approach) with our consultant, Dr. Bloomberg. During the first academic quarter, Dr. Bloomberg facilitated the EAA Protocol with each IMPACT Team. During the second quarter, the Principal or a Division Chair facilitated this protocol with each IMPACT Team. Dr. Bloomberg provided on-the-spot coaching to our administrative facilitators. By providing effective feedback and job coaching, the expertise of the consultant was scaled out to LTHS administrators. During the third quarter, a teacher from the IMPACT Team facilitated the protocol with coaching from the consultant. During the fourth quarter, a second teacher from the IMPACT Team facilitated the protocol with coaching from the Division Chair or principal, who was receiving feedback on coaching from the consultant.

By providing education, opportunity for practice, effective feedback, and additional opportunity to apply the feedback to their practice, the ten teams have been thoroughly supported in implementing this protocol. They not only understand the purpose of their IMPACT Team meetings, but also have demonstrated that they can collectively carry these meetings out on behalf of students.

TIMELINE FOR BUILDING PROFESSIONAL CAPACITY: Evidence-Analysis-Action Protocol		
Quarter	Facilitator	Coach (Providing Feedback to the Facilitator)
Qtr. 1	Consultant	NA
Qtr. 2	Principal *or* Department Chair	Consultant
Qtr. 3	Teacher 1	Consultant
Qtr. 4	Teacher 2	Principal *or* Department Chair

Next Steps

After intense practice with the EAA Protocol, the team members, who have worked with the consultant for the last 2 years, will collaborate with an assigned administrator to teach their larger course team the protocol. They will apply this protocol quarterly throughout the 2016–2017 school year, thereby facilitating a structured conversation around student learning that results in a differentiated instructional action plan.

During the 2016–2017 school year, LTHS will begin the process again with eight new targeted teams. During their initial year of work with the consultant, they will align their curriculum to the Common Core, develop aligned and appropriately rigorous formative and summative assessments, and select and implement research-based instructional practices.

2016–2017: New Teams	
Department	**Team**
Fine Arts	Spanish I Spanish II
Language Arts	English I IPC
Math	Algebra II
Science	Physics
Social Studies	Psychology
Special Education	PSD
IMPACT Team Focusing on New Protocols	
Science	Chemistry
Social Science	World History

> "*Every successful initiative that I have been a part of during my 13 years as a school leader has involved a methodical and gradual approach to implementation. In approximately six months, we have evolved from the beginning stages of learning the Impact Team model (and associated protocols) with Dr. Bloomberg, to now having 15 LTHS faculty members from a variety of content areas who can effectively facilitate the Evidence-Analysis-Action protocol. Utilizing a gradual release approach, we will be able to have 8 self-sustaining Impact Teams during the 2016–17 school year, which will continue to build capacity with the model and protocols as we move forward at LTHS.*"
>
> —Dr. Brian Waterman, Principal

Finally, LTHS will support continued work with two current IMPACT Teams. These teams will spend the year learning and applying four additional protocols with Dr. Bloomberg: Calibration/Collaborative Scoring, Lesson Study, and Evidence Walks, and Microteaching. The two Model Teams will then serve as internal experts, who will be able to teach these remaining protocols to all teams in the future.

VIDEO DESCRIPTIONS

Chapter 7: Leading Model Teams

Overview: The videos in this chapter illustrate the power of the Model Team Approach in building Impact Team Capacity.

	Video 7-1: The Model Team Approach, Lyons Township High School, La Grange, IL	Dr. Brian Waterman, principal of LTHS, gives his perspective in launching Model Impact Teams.
	Video 7-2: The Model Team Approach, Joplin Schools, Joplin, MO	Sarah Stevens, Director of Professional Learning for The Core Collaborative and former Director of Curriculum and Instruction for Joplin Schools, gives her perspective on launching Model Teams in her former district.
	Video 7-3: The Model Team Approach, East Central BOCES, Limon, CO	Sharon Daxton-Vorce, Impact Team Coach and Coordinator of Professional Learning for the EC BOCES, discusses how their team built capacity with the Model Team Approach.
	Video 7-4: The Model Team Approach, Reeds Spring School District, Reeds Spring, MO	Jodi Gronvald, principal at Reeds Spring Intermediate, discusses getting started with Impact Teams.

APPENDICES

Appendix A

Purposeful Protocols

Evidence • Analysis • Action

Analyzing Student Work

EAA IMPACT TEAM MEETING PROTOCOL

Purpose

Impact Team meetings are rigorous, highly efficient, and result in evidence-based decision making. The three-step process for analyzing student work, **E**vidence • **A**nalysis • **A**ction (EAA), is followed for the meeting to:

- Stay focused
- Stimulate collaborative inquiry
- Build knowledge
- Share knowledge
- Result in collective action

Time

- 40–60 minutes

Resources

- Access to shared team folder—unpacked standard, success criteria, learning progressions, team meeting notes template
- Projection (if possible)

Materials

- Student work by learning group, including students' self-assessment, and success criteria for the learning intention

Step	Procedure	Time Allotment
1	**EVIDENCE: Team members prepare evidence based on the following previously agreed-upon criteria**	**5 Minutes**
	• Evidence is based on the success criteria of the product or performance aligned to focus standard(s) • Evidence provides a window into students' thinking • Evidence is disaggregated into three to four performance levels (exemplary, proficient, progressing, not yet) • Evidence is prepared for discussion prior to Impact Team meeting • Evidence includes diverse data (formative assessment, self- and peer assessment, goal setting sheets, etc.)	
2	**ANALYSIS: Team members engage in collaborative inquiry based on the evidence.**	**5 minutes per level (total 15–20 minutes)**
	• Analysis is based on success criteria • Analysis is by each performance level • Strengths and next learning steps are based on root cause or why • Next learning steps are determined for each performance level • Next learning steps must reflect the learning progression	
3	**ACTION: Team members collaboratively determine strategic action for each performance level based on the evidence and analysis**	**5 minutes per level (total 15–20 minutes)**
	• Team creates instructional plan using clusters of high impact strategies for each performance level • Team creates SMARTER goals for each performance level • Team implements and monitors action plan for all learners • Team reflects on instructional plan to determine impact on learning • Team records collective actions that have the greatest impact	

CHECK-IN AND CASE STUDY PROTOCOL

Purpose

During the learning cycle, Impact Teams check in with each other frequently to share successes and challenges based on their collective action agreements, after the team uses the EAA Team Meeting protocol to analyze student work. Rather than waiting until the end of the unit, they share artifacts, experiences, and student input and make timely corrections as needed. One successful practice we use is having each teacher choose students who are representative of a learning group and/or demographic group (e.g., long-term ELL student, at-risk student, gifted and talented student, etc.). They use these students' work as representative samples (case study) to make generalizations about teaching effectiveness. They study the same students throughout the school year

- to monitor student progress,
- to share successful strategies,
- to share challenges,
- to make midcourse corrections to ensure student progress, and
- to make generalizations about student subgroups.

Time

- 20–30 minutes

Materials

- Student and teacher artifacts

Step	Procedure	Time Allotment
1	**Evidence**	**5–10 minutes**
	Team identifies evidence or samples of student work based on representative learning groups based on the EAA Team Meeting Protocol.	
2	**Analysis**	**5–10 minutes**
	Team analyzes evidence based on strengths/obstacles for each sample based on each student group.	
3	**Action**	**5–10 minutes**
	Team takes collective action by making midcourse corrections if necessary. Team archives effective practice for future.	

Check-In and Case Study Template

Artifact Descriptions:
Success Criteria:

Student Group(s)	Evidence (What is it?)	Analysis (What were the learning strengths?)	Action (What is the next step: *continuation? midcourse correction?*)
Demographic Group			
Demographic Group			

LESSON STUDY PROTOCOL

Purpose

Impact Teams use lesson study to improve instructional effectiveness specific to the formative assessment process. It is a collaborative learning process in which teacher teams examine their practice from the planning stage through teaching, observing, and critiquing. The team creates a detailed lesson plan that one teacher teaches and the others observe. The focus of the observation is on the students' responses rather than the teacher's actions. Based on the evidence the team revises the lesson. The teachers can then go and teach the lesson another time after making the appropriate adjustments. *Note: Teachers usually engage in lesson study two to three times per year with a focus on implementation of the formative assessment process (EAA Classroom Protocol).*

Time

- 45–60 minutes for developing lessons
- 30–60 minutes for observing lessons / Evidence
- 40–60 minutes for analyzing lessons / Analysis
- 10–20 minutes for refinement and reflection / Action

Resources

- Curricular materials for lesson development
- Release time for team members to observe lesson
- Projection (if possible)

Materials

- Copy of lesson plan, template for recording observation—teacher actions and student responses

Step	Procedure	Time Allotment
1	**Lesson Planning**	45–60 minutes
	<ul><li>Team plans lesson to observe.</li><li>Team agrees on the teacher actions/strategies.</li><li>Team reaches consensus on the intended student behaviors for each teacher action (observable behaviors).</li><li>Team identifies possible difficulties students might have.</li><li>Team determines the intervention for each difficulty.</li><li>Team constructs observation template that has agreed-upon teacher actions identified with a space to record student behaviors for each teacher action.</li></ul>	
2	**Evidence: Team Observation**	30–60 minutes
	<ul><li>Team uses observation template to record student behaviors.</li><li>Team does not interact with students.</li><li>This can be recorded if classroom coverage is not available.</li></ul>	

(Continued)

(Continued)

Step	Procedure	Time Allotment
3	**Analysis: Lesson Analysis / Reflection**	**40–60 minutes**
	• Teams use the evidence of student behaviors to analyze what parts of the lesson were effective (why?). • Teams use the evidence of student behaviors to analyze what parts of the lesson were ineffective (why not?).	
4	**Action: Lesson Refinement and Reflection**	**10–20 minutes**
	• Team refines the lesson based on the analysis. • Final Reflection.	

Guiding Questions / Evidence:

- How will the team determine if students were clear in what they were learning?
- How will the team know if the lesson impacted learning?

Guiding Questions / Analysis:

- How did the team discuss the subject/topic? Did they refer to how students learn the subject/topic and the essential elements of the subject/topic? In what ways?
- In what ways did the team link their lesson to their broader learning intention?

Guiding Questions / Action:

- Revision: What did the team use to record revisions to the lesson? How will the revisions ensure success for students?
- Reflection: Was the conversation open to all participants? For example, if the lesson was observed, did the entire team observe it? If the lesson was based on a textbook, was everyone on the team familiar with the textbook? Were less experienced participants able to ask questions or propose ideas?
- Reflection: How did the team members reflect on their teaching practice? On student learning? On the group process? How did the group record its process? How did the group keep track of ideas and revisions to the lesson?

Explore these templates and resources on the Columbia Teachers College website:

http://www.tc.columbia.edu/centers/lessonstudy/

MICROTEACHING PROTOCOL

Purpose

Microteaching is organized practice teaching that provides Impact Team members the opportunity to try out small parts of lessons and/or strategies specific to the formative assessment process and receive constructive feedback for improvement. The mini lessons are recorded prior to the Impact Team meetings based on a strategy or approach that the team wants to learn—this need comes up typically while the team is using the EAA Meeting Protocol. The team observes the video and provides feedback to the practice teacher. Then each member of the team has an opportunity to try the technique observed. The team then summarizes what was learned after the session.

Time

- 45–50 minutes

Resources

- Mini-lesson preparation by the practice teacher
- Video Recording

Materials

- Identified focus for feedback (criteria) / EAA Classroom Protocol

Step	Procedure	Minutes
1	**Evidence • Video Observation**	5–10
	<ul><li>Team determines "lens" for observation.</li><li>Criteria from the EAA Classroom Protocol can provide a lens for observation.</li><li>Team observes practice teacher engaging students in a specific formative assessment practice.</li><li>Team takes notes in connection with the criteria used for observing.</li></ul>	

(Continued)

(Continued)

Step	Procedure	Minutes
2	**Analysis**	**15**
	Appreciative Feedback	5
	• Team names specific strengths associated with criteria for observation.	
	Self-Assessment and Clarification	5–10
	• Practice teacher reflects on the lesson after appreciative feedback. • Reflection may include strengths and possible next steps. • Team asks clarifying questions prior to team practice.	
3	**Action**	**20**
	Team Practice	**10**
	• Team members practice the strategy observed with a partner or triad based on a future unit. • Each team member gets an opportunity to practice.	
	Feedback Summary	**5–10**
	• Team collaboratively identifies one or two ways to improve teaching technique based on practice and feedback.	

CALIBRATION PROTOCOL

Purpose

To ensure that all members of the Impact Team are accurately scoring student work and that they are consistent in their scoring, creating inter-rater reliability. This protocol also ensures that the team's definition of *proficient* is the same.

Time

- 40–60 minutes
- This could also take extended periods of time depending on complexity of the student work.

Resources

- Copies of the success criteria and/or rubrics

Materials

- Copies of unscored student work from different learning groups (single copies of up to eight different samples)
- Sticky notes
- Different colored pens/pencils

Step	Procedure	Time Allotment
EVIDENCE		
1	**Review the Evidence**	**5 minutes**
	• Team members review the rubrics and/or success criteria and the assignment.	
ANALYSIS		
2	**Independent Scoring**	**5 minutes**
	• Each team member scores one piece of student work without discussion. • Score is written on a sticky note on the back of the work.	
3	**Pass the Piece**	**10–20 minutes**
	• Team members pass the piece of student work on to a new member who then scores the work. • That score is then added to the back of the work. • Continue this process until each team member has scored each piece of work.	
4	**Discuss the Differences**	**10 minutes**
	• The team discusses the differences in the scores. • Team members explain why they scored it the way they did, referencing the rubric and/or success criteria. • This continues until all pieces of student work have been discussed or until the team feels they are consistently applying the rubric/success criteria.	
ACTION		
5	**Revise the Rubric**	**5–10 minutes**
	• The team makes any needed changes to the rubric/success criteria to reflect the new understanding	
6	**Clarify for Student Understanding**	**5–10 minutes**
	• The team discusses ways to ensure that all students understand and can use the rubric/success criteria for self- and peer assessment. • The team chooses pieces of student work for examples of the success criteria and/or levels in the rubric.	

EVIDENCE WALKS PROTOCOL

Purpose

To develop a shared understanding of what high-quality instruction looks like specific to the formative assessment process. This protocol can be used to scale up expertise around the formative assessment five core practices districtwide or for a school site. To build a culture of relational trust, instructional leadership teams are invited to participate in the evidence walk.

Time

- Half Day (3–5 classes—host chooses the classes to visit and the focus)

Resources

- EAA Classroom Protocol

Materials

- Smart phones for video, photographs, and audio
- Note Taker
- Time Keeper

Step	Procedure	Time Allotment
1	**Setting the Stage**	5 minutes
	• Team members review the EAA classroom protocol. • Discuss the following question full group: What does it look like to learn implement and model the core practices of the formative assessment process?	
2	**Focus of Learning**	5 minutes
	• How do students know what they are learning, why they are learning it, and what success looks like? • Briefly discuss what you would hope to hear and see regarding this focus.	
3	**Overview of Lessons and Context**	10–15 minutes
	• Host shares details regarding class contexts (class size, relevant student information). • Host shares the learning intentions and success criteria each teacher or school site is focusing on. • Host shares strategies specific to the EAA classroom protocol (the formative assessment process).	

Step	Procedure	Time Allotment
	• Host shares what questions they are curious about specific to the formative assessment process (e.g., We have been wondering about this . . . . We have been trying this . . . . We want to know what you think about this . . . .) • Group defines what questions they will ask students when entering the classroom (e.g., What are you learning? How do you know you will be successful? Why are you learning this?)	
4	**Review Norms for Observation**	**5 minutes**
	• Observations recorded in writing, photos, audio, and so on. • Evidence is based on what participants see and hear. • Descriptive and nonjudgmental	
EVIDENCE		
5	**Observations**	**10–15 minutes (each class; this can vary)**
	• Define task observed • Describe what students are saying and doing • Describe what teacher is saying or doing • Environmental Scaffolds	
ANALYSIS		
6	**Observation Analysis (Debrief)**	**5–10 minutes**
	• Sharing of observations (jig saw) • What were the students able to do? What are their strengths? • Analyze the picture this evidence presents	
ACTION		
7	**Responding to Host**	**5–10 minutes**
	• Respond to host's questions • Determine next steps for professional learning • Discuss any questions raised • Set goals for the individual and/or group	

Student-Centered Evidence Walks

Date: _____

Team: _____

Focus of Learning: (e.g., *How do students know the goals for their learning? Do the students understand and use success criteria to guide their learning?*)

Class 1	Class 2
What is the task?	What is the task?
What is the teacher saying and doing?	What is the teacher saying and doing?
What are the students saying and doing?	What are the students saying and doing?

Norms

Observations	Debrief
• Nonevaluative (descriptive observation, not judgment)	• Evidence-based • Listen
Climate	**Classroom Interactions**
• Collaborative not competitive • Open to learning—honest • Respectful	• Interactions with students with permission of teacher • Nonintrusive • Attentive/reflective listeners

Note: Typically during evidence walks observers ask students the following questions:

- What are you learning today?
- How do you know you will be successful?
- What do you do when you are stuck? Among others.

UNPACKING FOR SUCCESS PROTOCOL

Purpose

Impact Teams meet to collaboratively get to know the standards at a deep level. Based on their collective understanding, they develop learning intentions and success criteria for the standards. They plan backwards from the learning intention to develop cohesive units, clarity for the students, and to connect daily instruction to the learning intention (standard):

- Deeply understand the standards
- Determine big ideas
- Develop learning intentions, possible products and performance for success criteria
- Interpret the standard in student-friendly language
- Connect daily instruction to the learning intention
- Develop formative assessment rubrics and/or checklists

Time

- 40–60 minutes

Resources

- State standards, district curriculum guides, state and district resources for understanding the standards
- Unpacking template
- Laptops connected to the internet to access information about the standard
- Wiki-Teacher, PARCC Evidence Tables, Tulare County Bookmarks, etc.
- Common Core Companion (Burke)
- Web's DOK (Depth of Knowledge) and/or Karen Hess' Matrix (Bloom's and Web's DOK, see http://www.nciea.org/cgi-bin/pubs page.cgi?sortby=pub_date)
- Projection (if possible)

Step	Procedure	Time Allotment
1	**Research the Standard**	**10–15 minutes**
	• Each Impact Team member reads a different resource on the standard. • Each team member then shares what they learned about the standard.	
2	**Determine Skills and Concepts**	**5 minutes**
	Skills	Concepts	

(Continued)

(Continued)

Step	Procedure	Time Allotment
3	**DOK and Rationale**	**5–10 minutes**
	• Using Web's DOK and/or Hess' Matrix, collaboratively determine the rigor of the standard (ceiling) • Consider the context (e.g., complexity of text /task, etc.)	
4	**Learning Progression (notes)**	**5 minutes**
	• Determine the standards involved in the progressions (standards that come in the grades before and in the grades after). • Discuss and note the change in expectations.	
5	**Relevance for Students**	**5–10 minutes**
	Big Idea Essential Question	
	Relevant Products or Performances	
6	**Develop Key Competencies**	**10–15 minutes**
	• Determine what the necessary skills and knowledge are for students to be proficient (successful) for this standard. • These ingredients/components are the tools that enable students to self- and peer assess. • Determine possible products or performances specific to the standard (e.g., graphic organizer, debate, discussion, etc.).	

Unpacking for Success Template

(1) Research Standard(s): Use this box for your notes.

(2) Determine the Skills and Concepts	
Skills	Concepts

(3) DOK and Rationale

(4) Learning Progression (notes)

(5) Relevance	
Big Idea(s)	Essential Question(s)

Relevant Products or Performances

(6) Develop Key Competencies (Learning intentions and success criteria are developed from these competencies.)

EVIDENCE • ANALYSIS • ACTION CLASSROOM PROTOCOL

The Impact Team Model (ITM) uses a classroom protocol (EAA Classroom) to operationalize the five core formative assessment practices. The classroom protocol has three phases:

1. Evidence
   - Learning Intentions
   - Success Criteria

2. Analysis
   - Self and Peer Assessment
   - Feedback

3. Action
   - Goal Setting
   - Revision

The three phases combine to create a cycle of learning in which students and teachers partner together during each phase. Each phase of the protocol supports teachers in deep implementation of the formative assessment process. The length of each learning cycle is determined by curricular goals and student need. Impact Teams ensure that students know what they are expected to know, understand, and do by designing learning cycles in incremental steps to build student knowledge and skills.

EAA Classroom Success Criteria (NY = *Not Yet,* S = *Sometimes, U = Usually)*	NY	S	U
(1) EVIDENCE			
Learning Intentions (LI) and Success Criteria (SC)			
Teacher explains and models using samples of student work or exemplars to illustrate the success criteria of the perspective product or performance.			
Students can articulate the learning intention and success criteria.			
Students engage in coconstruction of the success criteria with their classmates and teacher.			
Students can identify success criteria in student work samples and exemplars.			
Students reflect regularly using essential questions connected to big ideas.			

EAA Classroom Success Criteria *(NY = Not Yet, S = Sometimes, U = Usually)*	NY	S	U
Assessment Tools			
Rubrics and or checklists reflect the learning intention and success criteria aligned to focus learning progression/standard(s).			
Exemplars are annotated by the success criteria and are visible to students (notebooks, learning management system [LMS], classroom environment).			
Samples of student work are used so students can practice applying the success criteria (varying degrees of proficiency).			
(2) ANALYSIS			
Peer and Self-Assessment, Feedback			
Teacher models how to self- and peer assess using samples of student work. Teacher thinks aloud while modeling the process.			
Teacher models how to give and receive evidence-based feedback in a respectful manner. Feedback language stems and frames are posted for students to use during this process.			
Students use rubrics/checklists when engaged in self- and peer assessment.			
Students get regular practice applying the success criteria.			
Students can identify success criteria in others' work.			
Students can give feedback based on the success criteria in a respectful manner.			
Students engage in reflective dialogue with peers and teacher based on rubrics/checklist.			
Students get regular feedback from teacher to lift the accuracy of their self- and peer assessments.			
(3) ACTION			
Goal Setting, Revision, Feedback			
Teacher models how to set learning goals, make action plans, revise student work, and reflect using evidence-based feedback.			
Students reflect on their strengths and next steps based on feedback from peer and self-assessment and teacher.			
Students create personal learning goals based on feedback.			
Students revise assessment product based on feedback tied to rubric/checklist.			
Students keep track of their progress and mastery of Focus Standards (they have a way to organize their learning).			

LADDER OF FEEDBACK CLASSROOM PROTOCOL

Topic:
Feedback from:
Feedback for:
My feedback will focus on:

VALUE **What do you see in this work that you find to be particularly impressive, innovative, or strong?** → I like how you . . . → As a reader, it was enjoyable when you . . . → I was impressed with . . . → _____ was a strength.	Your comments
CLARIFY **Are there aspects or specific parts of this work that you don't believe you have understood as well as you could have?** → Can you help me understand . . . → Can you clarify . . . → I wonder why . . .	Your comments
SUGGESTIONS FOR NEXT TIME **Based on our Rock Star success criteria, do you have specific suggestions on how to address the concerns you identified above?** → I think focusing on _____ would really help you improve. → Being more descriptive with _____ would really help. → Developing _____ would really strengthen _____.	Your comments

OTHER CONCERNS OR ISSUES	Your comments
Do you detect some potential problems or challenges within the work? Do you disagree with some part of the work? Was the evidence and analysis consistent? → I respectfully disagree with . . . → When your writing is complete, I would make sure . . . → Do you think _____ will prevent you from having the best final product possible?	

Reflect and Create a Goal

Based on the feedback you received and our success criteria, what is <u>one specific aspect</u> of your work that you want <u>to improve on</u>?

_____

_____

_____

_____

What specifically <u>will you do</u> to achieve your goal?

_____

_____

_____

_____

PLANNING FRAMES FOR STUDENT PEER REVIEW

Planning Frames: Goal Setting

To make progress at _____ I could . . .

How I plan to do this is . . .

I will do this by _____.

I will know I am successful by using the following evidence:

Planning Frame: Peer Assessment

1. Is your goal doable?

2. How did you determine the time frame to accomplish your goal?

3. How will you know you are improving?

4. What evidence are you using to show others that you are making progress?

5. Explain the models of success you are using to help you achieve your goal?

6. Who do you think could help you reach your goal?

Appendix B

Math Unpacking Example

Unpacking for Success • Third-Grade Mathematics

Notice how this third-grade teacher team adapted the unpacking template to fit their need. Please feel free to adapt the template in any way that your team sees fit.

(1) Research Standard(s): Copy the standard and use this box for your notes.		
3.OA.A.3 Use multiplication and division within 100 to solve word problems in situations involving equal groups, arrays, and measurement quantities, e.g., by using drawings and equations with a symbol for the unknown number to represent the problem. ***This standard is in a cluster that is a critical area of focus.**		
(2) Rigor: Identify where the standard falls (conceptual, procedural, application) and what is needed for instruction:		
Conceptual Understanding	*Procedural Fluency*	*Application*
This is a conceptual cluster, and this standard does not need to be taught in isolation. The other standards within the cluster are meant to accompany this standard.		Students must develop their understanding of multiplication and division through contextual situations.

(Continued)

(Continued)

Students will solve multiplication and division problems that include equal groups, arrays, and the area model. Students need the opportunity to use concrete objects, create drawings, and write equations that represent the situations within the problems.		

(3) Determine the Skills and Concepts

Skills (What students have to do)	Concepts (What students must know)
Use Solve	Multiplication and Division ● within 100 Word problems involving ● equal groups ● arrays ● measurement quantities

Examples (if provided in the standard):

e.g., by using drawings and equations with a symbol for the unknown number to represent the problem

(4) Cognitive Rigor

DOK of Content Standard (without MPS)	DOK when intersected with the Mathematical Practices Claims identified by SBAC and PARCC
DOK: 1, 2 Note: notice how the cognitive rigor increases when MPS are integrated with the content standard.	SBAC Claim 2: MPS 1, 5, 7, 8—DOK 1, 2, 3 SBAC Claim 4: MPS 2, 4, 5—DOK 1, 2, 3, 4 PARCC: MPS 1 and 4

(5) Mathematical Practices related to this Standard

(Examples of how students will use the MPS with the identified content standard.)

MPS1: Solve different types of problems to find the product and discover the meaning of multiplication.

MPS 2: Use quantitative reasoning to determine what is happening in contextual situations.

MPS 3: Justify solutions and reasoning by constructing arguments about the use of concrete objects and critique the reasoning of others by comparing their models to others.

MPS 4: Use concrete objects and models (arrays, area models, equations, measurement quantities) to represent and solve real-world problems.

MPS 5: Use tools/objects to create arrays, model situations with equal groups, measurement tools, etc.

MPS 6: Develop an understanding of vocabulary words *multiplication, product, factors, quotient, divisor, dividend.*

MPS 7: Students will discover the patterns that exist, use the properties (commutative, associative, distributive) to develop understanding of multiplication and division facts.

MPS 8: Use the patterns in multiplication and the relationships of facts to become fluent in basic facts (multiplication and division).

(6) Learning Progression—Vertical and Horizontal Coherence		
Prerequisites—Previous Standards *(Standards that support identified standard)*	**Horizontal— Current Grade** *(Standards that support identified standard)*	**Extended—Future Standards** *(Standards that will require identified standard)*
2.OA.C.3 2.OA.C.4	3.OA.A.1 3.OA.A.2 3.OA.A.4 3.OA.B.5 3.OA.B.6 3.MD.C.7 3.MD.D.8	4.OA.A.2 4.OA.A.3 4.NBT.B.5 4.NBT.B.6 4.MD.A.3

(7) Relevance and Essential Questions: What's the point? Why is this important?	
Big Idea Statements (What students need to discover)	Essential Questions (Drive Intellectual Curiosity—the hook)
Multiplication and division are inverse operations. Unitizing makes a group into one unit. Arrays are multiplication tools that visualize the decomposition of factors.	How are multiplication and division related? Why is it possible to break apart a factor in many ways and the product is the same?

Relevance
Area/Measurement   • Construction   • Design   • Gardening   • Sewing

(Continued)

(Continued)

Equal groups

- Cooking
- Sharing /dividing supplies among participants
- Business—packaging supplies

Comparisons

- Statistics and probability
- Combinations

Future Math Courses

- Exponents
- Scientific notation
- Simplifying and solving equations/inequalities
- Combinations
- Permutations
- Matrices
- Vectors

(8) Develop Key Competencies at the standard level: Students should be able to (end of year standard)

Unit:

Solve multiplication/division word problems within 100 that involve equal groups.

Solve multiplication/division word problems within 100 that involve arrays.

Solve multiplication/division word problems within 100 that involve measurement quantities.

Use a strategy/model to represent a real-world situation that involves multiplication/division.

Weekly/Daily lessons:

Read and correctly interpret word problem.

Estimate a solution.

Identify the operation(s) needed to find solution and use at least one of the following:

- Use equal group to solve multiplication/division problems within 100.
- Use array to solve multiplication/division problems within 100.
- Use measurement quantities to solve multiplication/division problems within 100.
- Use repeated addition/subtraction to solve multiplication/division problems within 100.

Verify solution by using another method to solve problem.

Includes correct units in final solution.

Appendix C

Formative Assessment Examples

This is an example of a rubric that can be used across content areas with a focus on strengthening students' ability to develop claims, support claims with evidence, and analyze the evidence. This rubric is meant to be used across units so students get multiple chances to practice until they are proficient with the skill, Claim• Evidence • Reasoning (CER).

CLAIM • EVIDENCE • REASONING (CER)

CATEGORY	Developing	Progressing	Proficient
Claim: A statement that responds to the questions asked or the problem posed.	Does not make a claim, or makes an inaccurate claim.	Makes an accurate but incomplete claim.	Makes an accurate claim.
Evidence: Textual, mathematical, or scientific evidence to support the claim.	Does not provide any evidence, or only provides inappropriate evidence (that does not support the claim).	Provides appropriate, but insufficient evidence to support the claim. May include some inappropriate evidence.	Provides appropriate and sufficient evidence to support the claim (2–3 strong examples).
Reasoning: Uses explanations to show why the evidence supports the claim.	Does not provide reasoning, or only provides reasoning that does not link evidence to the claim.	Provides reasoning that links the claim and evidence. Repeats the evidence and/or includes some explanation, but is not sufficient.	Provides reasoning that links evidence to the claim. Includes a solid explanation and/or uses solid mathematical or scientific principles.

My strengths:

My next steps:

Timeline:

LINEAR EQUATIONS EXAMPLE

Carol Cronk, an Impact Team consultant for the Core Collaborative, developed this model to illustrate the use of learning progressions as a support for developing learning intentions and success criteria for three tasks aligned to the same standard with a focus on linear equations.

Solve linear equations with rational number coefficients, including equations whose solutions require expanding expressions using the distributive property and collecting like terms. *(CCSS.Math.Content.8.EE.C.7.b)*

Learning Progressions

Emerging	Solve one- and two-step equations with whole number coefficients.
Below Basic	Solve multiple-step equations with whole number coefficients.
Basic	Solve multiple-step equations with rational number coefficients.
Proficient	Solve linear equations with rational number coefficients requiring the use of distributive property and collecting like terms.
Advanced Proficient	Create and solve linear equations with rational number coefficients requiring the use of distributive property and collecting like terms that come from contextual situations.

Example 1:

Today we will solve multiple-step equations with whole number (or rational number) coefficients.

Task: Solve $5x+1 = 2x+7$ in two ways: symbolically, the way you usually do with equations, and also with pictures of a balance. Show how each step you take symbolically is shown in the pictures. *(Illustrative Mathematics)* DOK 1, 2

SMP 1: Explain correspondences between equations, verbal descriptions, tables, and graphs or draw diagrams of important features and relationships, graph data, and search for regularity or trends. Check answers to problems using a different method.

Success Criteria:

- Solve the equation algebraically.
- Set up a picture of the equation using a balance.

- Show the steps needed to solve the equation keeping the equation balanced.
- Compare answers.

Example 2:

Today we are comparing two ways to solve a linear equation.

Task: What issues arise when you try to solve the equation $2 = 2x-4$ using pictures? Do the same issues arise when you solve this equation symbolically? *(Illustrative Mathematics)* DOK 1, 2

SMP1: Explain correspondences between equations, verbal descriptions, tables, and graphs or draw diagrams of important features and relationships, graph data, and search for regularity or trends. Check answers to problems using a different method.
   Success Criteria:

- Decide on a model for representing the equation.
- Solve the equation step-by-step and note what issues are encountered.
- Solve the equation symbolically.
- Discuss the similarities and differences of the issues encountered when solving.

Example 3:

Today we are creating linear equations that have one, many, or no solutions.

Task: Make up a linear equation that has no solutions. What would happen if you solved this equation with pictures? How is this different than an equation that has infinitely many solutions? *(Illustrative Mathematics)* DOK 1, 2, 3

SMP 2: Attend to the meaning of quantities, not just how to compute them, and knowing and flexibly using different properties of operations and objects.

SMP 3: Use stated assumptions, definitions, and previously established results in constructing arguments. Make conjectures and build a logical progression of statements to explore the truth of the conjectures.

Success Criteria:

- Determine what makes an equation have no solutions.
- Create an equation that has no solutions.
- Determine what makes an equation that has infinite solutions.
- Create an equation that has infinite solutions.
- Compare and contrast the two types of equations.

CONSTRUCTING VIABLE ARGUMENTS IN MATHEMATICS

This Mathematics Impact Team developed this math practice rubric to support students' ability to justify their conclusions, communicate them to others, and respond to the arguments of others. This rubric can be used across units of study.

Math Practice	Developing	Approaching	Proficient	Exceeds
Constructs viable arguments	With prompting and support, I can explain my thinking for the solution I found.	I can explain my thinking for the solution I found.	I can explain my own thinking and thinking of others with accurate vocabulary.	I can justify and explain, with accurate vocabulary, why others are correct. I can use multiple methods to justify my thinking.

READING ANCHOR 2 • INFORMATIVE

Anchor 2: Determine central ideas or themes of a text and analyze their development; summarize the key supporting details.

This Impact Team developed this rubric to mirror the readers they had in their fifth-grade class. Some readers were reading at the third-grade reading level (developing on this rubric), some readers were reading at the fourth-grade reading level (approaching on this rubric). The category (meets) represents where readers should be by the end of fifth grade.

Progression	Developing	Approaching	Meets
Lexile	450–790	770–980	770–980
F and P	N–P	Q–S	T–V
Key Ideas	• Can write a statement of the main idea.	• Can write a statement of the main idea. Main idea is usually inferred at this level.	• Can write a statement of each main idea (2). Main ideas are usually inferred at this reading level.
Details	• Can copy, paraphrase, or highlight 2–3 key details that support the main idea.	• Can copy, paraphrase, or highlight 2–3 key details that support the main idea.	• Can paraphrase 2–3 key details that support main idea one. • Can paraphrase 2–3 key details that support main idea two.
Summary	• Can write a brief explanation as to why the key details support the main idea.	• Can summarize the text. Summary must include the main idea of the text and the key details that support the main idea.	• Can summarize the text. Summary must include both main ideas of the text and the key details that support each main idea.

Possible Learning Intentions aligned to the assessment criteria (success criteria) from the rubric above.

- Today we are learning how to determine importance in text by writing a statement of the main idea.
- Today we are learning how to tell the difference between main ideas and key details.

- Today we are learning two different ways to find key details in a text that supports the article's main idea.
- Today we are learning how to determine what idea the author thinks is most important.
- Today we are learning how to determine the most important points in a text.
- Today we are learning that authors can have multiple main ideas and how to determine them when we read.
- Today we are learning how to summarize text by including the main ideas and key details that support them.

STORY RETELLING RUBRIC (RL.1.2)

This rubric was developed by PS 9 first-grade teachers in Staten Island, NY, as a scaffold for retelling stories. Students and teachers give feedback based on the success criteria in this rubric.

SUCCESS CRITERIA	I need help.	I tried my best, but need a little help.	I can do this by myself.
My beginning includes: • character names • setting • character feelings • transitional words ("first," "in the beginning")			
My middle includes: • the problem • character feelings • transitional words ("then," "next")			
My end includes: • the solution • how the character's feelings changed • the lesson the character learned • transitional words ("finally," "in the end")			

BEAST WORLD HISTORY WRITING RUBRIC

	Legend	Rock Star	Opening Act	Garage Band
BIG IDEA	Introduces a **compelling** claim that **addresses** the question with three different examples as themes and takes a **purposeful** position on an issue and introduce a counter claim.	Introduces a **precise** claim that **addresses** the question with three different examples and takes an **identifiable** position on an issue.	Introduces a **vague** claim **that does not fully address** the question with three or fewer examples and **attempts** to take a position on an issue.	Contains an **unidentifiable** claim that **does not address** the question **or take** a position on an issue.
EVIDENCE	Provides evidence that is **valid, convincing, and significant** with **citations** to support the claim and counter claim.	Provides evidence that is **valid, sufficient, and relevant** with **citations** to support the claim.	Provides evidence that is **not consistently valid or relevant** in an attempt to support the claim.	Provides **insufficient** evidence to support the claim and that is **incomplete, not valid, or irrelevant.**
APPLY/ ANALYZE	Words and phrases are **strategically** and **convincingly** used to explain why and how the evidence supports the claim and counter claim.	Words and phrases are **skillfully** used to **effectively** explain why and how the evidence supports that claim.	Words and phrases are **used with limited effectiveness** to connect the claim.	Few, if any, words and phrases are used to connect evidence to the claim.

	Legend	Rock Star	Opening Act	Garage Band
SIGNIFICANCE	A specific example from a later time is used to **clearly and convincingly** connect the importance of the past to the present.	A specific example from a later time is used to **clearly connect** the importance of the past to the present.	A specific example from life today is introduced but is **vague** in its connection of the importance of the past to the present.	An **unidentifiable** specific example from life today or connection of the importance of the past to the present.
TIES TOGETHER	Provides a conclusion that **convincingly** summarizes the claim.	Provides a conclusion that **effectively** summarizes the claim.	Provides a conclusion that **vaguely** summarizes the claim.	Provides an **unidentifiable** conclusion.

The Lyons Township High School World History Impact Team developed this rubric for the World History course. They adapted this rubric from *turnitin.com.* The rubric is aligned to WHST.1, the argumentative writing standard from the CCSS for ninth grade. The team used this rubric across all units of study so students had lots of opportunities to practice before receiving a grade. Students engaged regularly in peer review. Students would only focus on one to two categories of the rubric at a time.

U.S. HISTORY—ANALYSIS OF A POLITICAL CARTOON—STUDENT GROWTH RUBRIC—ALIGNED TO CCSS LITERACY STANDARDS

	NOVICE	DEVELOPING	PROFICIENT	EXPERT
Time and Place	The response **inaccurately identifies** the time period and place of the cartoon.	The response **accurately identifies** either the time period or place of the cartoon.	The response **accurately identifies** the time period and place of the cartoon.	The response **accurately and specifically identifies** the time period and place of the cartoon using content-specific vocabulary.
Author's Topic and Point of View	The response **does not** identify the topic of the cartoon *(the historical event or political issue depicted in the cartoon)* or the author's point of view.	The response **identifies** either the topic of the cartoon *(the historical event or political issue depicted in the cartoon)* or the author's point of view.	The response **accurately identifies** the topic of the cartoon *(the historical event or political issue depicted in the cartoon)* and the author's point of view.	The response **accurately and specifically identifies** the topic of the cartoon *(the historical event or political issue depicted in the cartoon)* and the author's point of view.
Explanation of Historical Context	The response does not explain the historical context surrounding the cartoon, or it is **not historically accurate.**	The response **explains** the historical context surrounding the cartoon with some inaccuracies.	The response **accurately explains** the historical context surrounding the cartoon.	The response **thoroughly explains** the historical context surrounding the cartoon, **pointing out the underlying political, economic, or international tensions of the time.**

	NOVICE	DEVELOPING	PROFICIENT	EXPERT
Identification and Explanation of Significant Artistic Elements	The response **does not point out** the author's use of symbols and captions and **does not explain** how these artistic elements are used to convey the author's point of view.	The response **points out** the author's use of symbols and captions and **explains** how these artistic elements convey the author's point of view. However, some elements **may be inaccurately or insufficiently explained.**	The response **identifies and explains** the author's use of symbols and captions, **pointing out** what the symbols represent and how they are used to convey the author's point of view.	The response **analyzes** the author's use of symbols, distortions, caricatures, and/or captions, **pointing out** what the artistic elements represent and how they are used to convey the author's point of view. **Additionally, the response identifies** use of irony, analogies, and/ or humor, **and explains** how these additional artistic elements strengthen the author's point of view.
Evaluation of Effectiveness	**No claim** is made to comment on the effectiveness of the cartoon. Name _____	**A claim** may comment on the effectiveness of the cartoon, but it may cite **inaccurate or insufficient evidence.** **Student Growth Assessment #** _____	**A claim** is made concerning the effectiveness of the political cartoon **and it is supported with evidence from the cartoon.** **Period** _____	**A claim** is made concerning the effectiveness of the political cartoon **and it is supported with strong evidence.**

This rubric was developed by the Lyons Township High School U.S. History Team and can be used across units to strengthen students' ability to analyze political cartoons.

Appendix D

Evidence • Analysis • Action (Team Meeting) Resources

IMPACT TEAM NOTES SCAFFOLD

This template has been developed to support the peer facilitator and team in using the Evidence • Analysis • Action (EAA) Team Meeting Protocol in analyzing quality evidence (student work based on a rubric or checklist, student voice data, etc.). The template has guiding questions embedded in the template to strengthen peer facilitation. Notice how the guiding questions in the "action" part of the template use the four sources of efficacy to guide teacher planning.

Focus Standard(s)

Relevance

Enduring Understanding / Big Idea:

Why is it important for students to learn this?

Teacher Name	Total # of Students	Exemplary	Proficient	Developing	Novice
Total					

Evidence/Success Criteria	Analysis	Action
Exemplary	Why were students successful?	What would take these students to another level?
		Content: Strategies:
Meeting: Success criteria from scoring guide:	Why were students successful?	What can we do to help them reach proficiency?
		Four sources of efficacy—How will you: • Reengage students with application of the success criteria? • Immerse students with models of success (exemplars, through inquiry, through coconstruction, from each other). • Create opportunities for quality, reliable feedback? Engage students to use the feedback? • Expand collaborative learning opportunities? Create learning partnerships?

Evidence/Success Criteria	Analysis	Action
Developing: One to two barriers (from being proficient)	Why was this challenging?	What actions can we take to help them progress to the next level?
One thing this group struggled with based on the criteria		Same As Above + One more strategy:
Novice: Biggest barrier	Why was this challenging?	What actions can we take to help them progress to the next level?
		Same As Above + • Learning Progression • Small Group Instruction—How often? Group size?

SMARTER Goals: Fractions

Exemplary	Proficient	Developing	Novice

Norms

Listen/ contribute	Prepared	Punctual	Focused

Final Notes

IMPACT TEAM NOTE SCAFFOLD

This example is based on a fourth-grade Impact Team meeting. The team was focusing on Main Idea (RI.4.2). Students had to write a paragraph using the following success criteria:

Read the article about Aztecs and then write a summary using the success criteria below:

- Write an accurate main idea statement.
- Determine at least three key details from the text that support the main idea of the whole text.
- Key details come from throughout the whole text.
- Write a brief explanation as to why the key details support the main idea.

Focus Standard(s)

RI.4.2: Determine the main idea of a text; recount the key details and explain how they support the main idea.

RI.3.5: Use text features and search tools (e.g., key words, sidebars, hyperlinks) to locate information relevant to a given topic efficiently. Standard from Grade 3.

Relevance

Enduring Understanding / Big Idea:

Good readers understand part to whole relationships in text. Good readers use text features to determine important information when they read.

Why is it important for students to learn this?

Researchers determine main ideas and key details when they take notes. When taking Cornell Notes understanding how to determine key information is important to be successful.

Teacher Name	Total # of Students	Exemplary	Proficient	Developing	Novice
Abraham	25	0	12/25	8/25	5/25
Stevens	28	0	14/28	6/28	8/28
Palacios	26	0	10/26	5/26	11/26
TOTAL	79	0	36/79	19/79	24/79

Evidence/Success Criteria	Analysis	Action
Exemplary	Why were students successful?	What would take these students to another level?
NA	NA	Content: Strategies:
Meeting: Success Criteria	Why were students successful?	What can we do to help them reach exemplary?
● *Writes an accurate main idea statement.* ● *Can determine at least three key details from the text that support the main idea of the whole text.* ● *Key details come from throughout the whole text.* ● *Writes a brief explanation about why the key details support the main idea.*	● *They could infer the main idea since it wasn't clearly stated.* ● *They saw connections between the key details and the overall main idea.* ● *They could sum up why the key details supported the main idea in a sentence.* ● *They obviously read the whole text since they pulled key details from the whole text.* ● *Some used a graphic organizer to plan their paragraph. They understood how the graphic organizer represented the structure of the text (part to whole)*	● *Have these students be a part of peer review opportunities with the students below proficiency.* ● *They could read a more complex text and practice the same success criteria.*
Developing: One to two barriers (from being proficient)	Why was this challenging?	What actions can we take to help them progress to the next level?
One thing this group struggled with based on the criteria: ● *Most didn't have three key details that supported the main idea. One detail didn't support the main idea.*	● *They may have not used the text features to find key details—all key details could have been identified by using the text features (subheading).* ● *They may not have read the whole article.*	Same As Above + ● *Engage in peer review with proficient students PLUS.* ● *Use a graphic organizer to track and organize their thinking.*
Novice: Biggest barrier	Why was this challenging?	What actions can we take to help them progress to the next level?
● *They weren't able to get the gist of the text.*	● *Text probably was too complex.* ● *They may not be able to find the focus of each paragraph or section—this is a second-grade expectation.*	Same As Above + ● *Read a lower lexile text and practice writing the focus for each section on Post-its.* ● *Small Group (guided reading) Instruction 3 times weekly for 2 weeks using post it strategy.*

SMARTER Goals: *(Specific, Measurable, Attainable, Realistic, Timely, Evaluate, Revise)*

Exemplary	Proficient	Developing	Novice
	55/79	14/79	10/79

Norms

Listen/contribute	Prepared	Punctual	Focused
X	X	X	X

Final Notes

Most of the students did well. We have a core group of students who are still reading about 2 years below grade level. We will be practicing the second-grade expectations on RI.2 with them for the next few weeks before trying a more complex text. We don't think they can find the focus of each section or paragraph. We will use small group instruction (guided reading using Post-its) as well. Some students in the developing category also will benefit from RI.2.2 practice.

We will check in in a week to see if our plan is working.

Here is an exemplar that was used during the formative assessment process to guide students.

The main idea of the informative text titled "Aztecs" describes the culture of the Aztecs. The first key detail describes the importance of religion to the Aztecs. Another key detail was that family life was important to this culture. Finally, the Aztecs were known for building great cities. They ruled Mexico for hundreds of years. Religion, family life, and great cities are all a part of the Aztec culture.

IMPACT TEAM PEER FACILITATION STEMS

Here are question stems for peer facilitation regarding the EAA Team Protocol for analyzing student work. Before coming to the Impact Team meeting, it is preferable that teachers guide students through the EAA classroom protocol (the formative assessment process). During the classroom session teachers should take anecdotal notes on the quality students' self- and peer assessments. This data will support teachers in making quality inferences in analyzing student work (Step 2). In addition, guiding students in self- and peer assessment prior to the Impact Team Meeting will reduce the time out of classroom instruction in scoring papers. Teachers should have students place their work in colored folders that represent each proficiency level after self- and peer review.

Step 1: Evidence

- Describe the task. What is the range or level of DOK of the task?
- What were the criteria for success? (check the rubric)
- Is there anything you would like to revise about the task for next time? If so, we can discuss at the end of the meeting.

Step 2: Analysis

- **Proficient and Advanced Students:** Why were the students successful with the criteria? What inferences can you make about why they were successful?

Hint: The team may want to discuss one criterion at a time for clarity.

- **Other Performance Levels:** Why did they miss that criterion point? What do you think is the root cause?

Hint: The team should only discuss reasons that they can control.

Step 3: Action

- How can we reengage students in understanding and applying the success criteria from the task?
- How can we ensure that students have varying models of success accessible to them?
- How can we ensure that students are getting evidence-based feedback in a timely manner? (teacher-to-student and peer-to-peer)

- How can we ensure that students are using the feedback to revise and set goals for their learning?
- How can we ensure that we are creating a culture that students are free to discuss their mistakes and learn from them?

Hint: Students who are struggling the most may benefit from more instruction and practice on skills and concepts from the learning progression below grade level. Small group instruction is beneficial to these students.

Appendix E

Impact Team Inquiry Cycles

EXAMPLE IMPACT TEAM CYCLE • HIGH SCHOOL

The Blue Wave High School World History Team wanted to have students take more ownership of their learning. They decided to do this by actively engaging students in quality peer and self-assessment and student goal setting. See how this team used the Impact Team protocols to guide their inquiry. This team meets every week for 50 minutes.

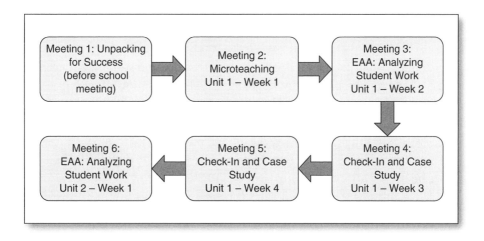

Meeting 1: Unpacking for Success: One week before their unit on Ancient Mesopotamia, the World History Team met to review the BEAST Writing Rubric they developed the previous year. This rubric was aligned to the argumentative writing standard WHST.1 from the Common Core Learning Standards. Students were engaged in inquiry throughout the unit using the following essential question:

EQ: Was ancient Mesopotamia a civilized or uncivilized place to live?

Students had to use multiple sources to defend their claim to this question. The World History Impact Team discussed how they would coconstruct the rubric criteria with the students during the first week of the unit. They decided to only focus on 2 sections of the rubric for the first assessment. The team determined that they wanted to learn more about co-construction of success criteria. One teacher (James) from the team volunteered to record himself so they could watch the video together during the next team meeting. They would use the Microteaching Protocol to guide their next team meeting.

Meeting 2: Microteaching: During the next meeting, and during the first week of the unit of study, James brought the video to the meeting for the team to observe. They watched the video of James coconstructing the success criteria from the BEAST writing rubric with one of his classes. The team named what James did well, and then they all discussed how they would do this in their own classroom in the next couple of days. The team decided to bring student work to the next team meeting based on just two sections of the BEAST rubric. They decided to use the EAA Meeting Protocol to the next meeting. Most teachers decided that they would engage the students in peer review prior to bringing the student work to the next meeting.

Meeting 3: EAA (Analyzing Student Work): During Meeting 3, the peer facilitator led the team in analyzing student work using the EAA protocol. They looked at student work from three different performance levels (students close to proficient, students progressing, and students in need of a lot of extra support). They developed a simple action plan regarding each performance group based on their discussion of student work. The team decided that students weren't very accurate in determining where they were at on the rubric. They decided to model and scaffold peer assessment through think-aloud before the next meeting. They decided to use the Check-In Protocol to guide their next team meeting.

Note: Best case scenario—Classroom teachers guide students in peer and self-assessment prior to the team meeting. This reduces scoring outside of classroom instruction and ensures that students get quality feedback in a timely manner. Teachers can guide students in placing their papers in colored folders that represent each performance level in preparation for the team meeting. This is also a time that teachers can give students feedback on their self- and peer assessments to ensure reliability and validity in student scoring.

Meeting 4: Check-In and Case Study: During Meeting 4, the team met to discuss how peer assessment went in their classroom. All the teachers shared what went well and what they would do differently next time. They all agreed that they needed to give more feedback to each partnership connected to the quality of the feedback students were giving to each other. The feedback students were giving wasn't specific enough. The team decided to teach the kids how to be more specific in their feedback to one another by modeling how to use the success criteria when using the ladder of feedback. The team decided to use the Check-In Protocol again to guide their next team meeting.

Meeting 5: Check-In and Case Study: During Meeting 5 the team shared how modeling giving feedback went using success criteria. The team unanimously decided that explicitly modeling giving feedback worked and it actually raised the quality of peer-to-peer feedback. They decided that they needed to do a lot more modeling of this in the future since it worked so well. The team decided that the students would write the essential question again, and they would bring student work to the next meeting to analyze.

Meeting 6: EAA (Analyzing Student Work): The team brought the final response from Unit 1 to the meetings. The peer facilitator guided the team through the EAA protocol. They realized immediately that most students made a ton of progress. They reflected why they made such an impact, and they determined the following:

- Coconstruction of the Success Criteria helped students own the rubric more.
- All the time spent modeling using the criteria from the rubric supported more students understanding the rubric criteria at deeper levels.
- The peer review, although not very good the first time, did support students in understanding what was expected of them; it seems to hold promise for continual use.

Appendix F

Impact Teams Pre-Assessment

Foundational Components	Not Yet	Sometimes	Always
Teaming to Learn			
We have established learning teams.			
Our teams agree and commit to their purpose.			
Our teams use protocols purposefully and responsively to guide team meetings.			
Our teams meet weekly for 45 to 60 minutes.			
Our teams have trained peer facilitators and they get ongoing job-embedded professional learning.			
Our teams get regular feedback based on the quality of their team meetings.			
Formative Assessment in Action			
Our classroom practices are based on the notion that teachers partner with students in the learning process—trust is high.			
Learning intentions and/or goals and success criteria are clearly communicated to students.			
Students are provided evidence-based feedback based on success criteria.			

(Continued)

(Continued)

Foundational Components	Not Yet	Sometimes	Always
Students use self- and peer assessment as sources of feedback.			
Students set goals and revise using the success criteria from rubric-bound formative assessments.			
Curriculum: Equitable, Viable, Coherent			
We have identified the focus standards.			
Our teams have determined the time needed to teach and learn the focus standards.			
Our teams have organized and sequenced the focus standards to maximize learning opportunities.			
Our teams have unpacked the focus standards and have developed student-friendly rubrics and/or checklists to aid in goal setting and revision.			
Our teams ensure that the curriculum is accessible to all students.			
Evidence to Inform and Act			
Our teams use multiple sources of student evidence to inform decision making.			
Our teams analyze specific evidence to take collective action.			
Strengthening Efficacy			
Our school understands the importance of strengthening efficacy.			
Our school intentionally plans for ways to build student, teacher, and collective efficacy.			

Appendix G

Team Trust Survey

HOW WELL DOES YOUR TEAM PRACTICE BEHAVIORS THAT BUILD TRUST?

Take a few moments to evaluate.

How to score:

    (1) Almost never (AN)

    (2) Occasionally (O)

    (3) Some of the time (ST)

    (4) Frequently (F)

    (5) Almost always (AA)

	1 AN	2 O	3 ST	4 F	5 AA
1. Do we keep agreements or renegotiate if we can't?	O	O	O	O	O
2. Do we have clear and explicit expectations regarding measurable goals for learning?	O	O	O	O	O
3. Do we act with mutually serving intentions without hidden agendas?	O	O	O	O	O
4. Do we share classroom strategies weekly/biweekly that are pertinent to increasing learning?	O	O	O	O	O

(Continued)

(Continued)

	1 AN	2 O	3 ST	4 F	5 AA
5. Do we speak our minds and tell the truth, even when others disagree?	O	O	O	O	O
6. Do we openly admit and take responsibility for the mistakes we have made?	O	O	O	O	O
7. Do we avoid gossiping or participating in unfair criticism about other people?	O	O	O	O	O
8. Do we have confidence in our abilities to keep up with the changing demands of our profession?	O	O	O	O	O
9. Do we acknowledge the skills and abilities of others?	O	O	O	O	O
10. Do we help each other learn new skills?	O	O	O	O	O

Add up all your scores for the above questions to come up with your score of the team.

Scoring

The highest possible score is 50, and the lowest is 10. The higher the score, the greater you perceive your team practices trust-building behaviors and the likelihood the team has effective working relationships.

How often your team practices trust-building behaviors:

10 to 15	Almost never. Create a goal to improve . There is serious room for improvement!
16 to 25	Occasionally, which damages trust within the team. Create a goal to improve.
26 to 35	Some of the time, which does not build sustainable trust. Create a goal to improve.
36 to 45	Frequently and are most likely have effective working relationships. Name what is working and replicate.
45 to 50	Almost always and are probably viewed as a highly effective team. Keep up the good work! How can you teach others to develop trust on their team?

Appendix H

Case Studies

INTRODUCTION TO CASE STUDIES

The Impact Teams case studies that follow provide an authentic record of three districts' experiences with the Impact Teams process. Each district is described demographically, and they identify their challenges and desired outcomes. The studies then go on to describe their learning journeys, including challenges, successes, and lessons learned.

We encourage schools and districts to share these case studies with their leadership teams to analyze a variety of real-world situations, to inform practice, to use as models, and to determine possible next steps. We also recommend using this simple case study format to chronicle your own journey with Impact Teams. And finally, this is living research, and we will be continually adding other case studies to the companion website as the work continues in other districts.

JOPLIN SCHOOLS

1. The Context: About the School/District

Joplin Schools is an urban-suburban community that spans 70 miles and is located in the southwest corner of Missouri. The Joplin School District serves around 7,600 students PK–12. There are 11 elementary schools, three middle schools, one high school and trade school, and one early childhood center. Of the 1,286 employees, 718 are certified staff; 49% of the certified staff hold a master's degree or higher.

2. Demographics

- Number of teachers: 718
- Number of students: 7,600
- Percentage of students on free or reduced lunch: 61%
- Percentage of limited English proficient students: 3%
- Percentage of special education students: 15%
- Any other relevant data: Average teacher experience is 10 years (http://joplinschools.org/Page/571)

3. The Challenge

In 2011, the city of Joplin was hit with an F5 tornado that was close to 1 mile wide and was on the ground for 13 miles, destroying six schools and hundreds of homes and businesses: it resulted in 161 lives being lost. It was the deadliest tornado in the United States since 1947 and resulted in being the most costly tornado recorded in U.S. history. As a result, people and businesses from all over the world generously responded to aide in the recovery of the community and in the Joplin Schools system. As the district began to rebuild, the Board of Education, administration, and the community committed to think in innovative ways and not just rebuild what had previously been. A team of district administrators, community members, parents, educators, and students decided to design schools to be collaborative, to have flexible spaces, and to engage students in learning anytime, anywhere. Innovation did not stop with just the bricks and mortar. For example, instead of textbooks, the decision was made to go 1:1 with Macbooks at the high school and focus on using open-ed resources to empower all learners to engage in college and career readiness and foster a passion for learning to become responsible and innovative citizens.

Along with the new spaces came a slew of new initiatives to help support the new environments and new thinking. The high school focused on project-based learning and authentic performance assessments and on becoming a career path high school. Middle schools were engaged in work around team planning, cross-curricular units of study, and increasing the rigor through the use of formative assessment. Elementary schools were heavily involved in curriculum work, using data-informed instruction, and designing tiered interventions to improve literacy. Needless to say, the district was hit with initiative fatigue and suffering from a lack of district-wide focus.

The challenge came full force with the implementation of the new Common Core State Standards (CCSS) and the drive to prepare students for the variety of new programs being designed at the high school. Teachers realized that they had become dependent on textbooks or programs. Totally absent was an aligned, engaging curriculum that was standards based. In addition, high-quality, standards-based formative assessments to measure student progress were not evident in most classrooms. The Instructional Services team reached out to Dr. Paul Bloomberg to begin work on curricular alignment and to create a model to monitor and measure student progress. The desire was to create a plan that would shift conversations away from just "the teaching" and balance the conversation toward "teaching and student learning." It was a team effort—the central office leadership team, principals, instructional coaches, and Dr. Bloomberg coconstructed a 3-year professional learning plan with an emphasis on developing self-regulated learners. Since the core of Impact Team is maximizing the formative assessment process, the goal became to implement the formative assessment process in all classrooms. The following objectives emerged.

Objective 1: Clarity

Develop a coherent curriculum in English Language Arts. We wanted it to build over time and transfer to other disciplines. The curriculum would create a context for learning so that teachers would set students up for success with authentic, relevant learning experiences. This curriculum was desperately needed, and we wanted a curriculum that would provide clarity for teacher teams and ultimately clarity for students.

Objective 2: Transferability

We wanted to ensure transferability of skills across content areas. It was important that when we engaged students in self- and peer assessment, reflection, and goal setting they were setting goals regarding standards that would prepare them for success in college, career, and civic life.

Objective 3: Equity

Ensure all students receive standards-based curriculum. Using the ELA/Literacy learning progressions was integral to our work regarding equity. We wanted our curriculum to suggest an intentional mapping about how to teach on earlier concepts to get deeper understanding. Since our students were at different levels, we wanted to make sure that there were multiple entry points into the curriculum. We also wanted to ensure that students were able to take ownership of their learning. The curriculum had to provide a guide for implementing the formative assessment process.

Impact Teams has helped teachers, myself, and the principal look at data differently. We ask each other now, "So how did this impact students?" or "What did the students that mastered it get that the others didn't?" We started to take a deeper look at the data; teachers then took it back to their instruction to revise or differentiate. It has become a process that we use that is continuous and ongoing. As a coach, I think Impact Teams helped me my first year get into conversations and then into classrooms. It opened up barriers for me to ask teachers how I could help or what we could do together to help the kids. It has become one of my favorite days where I get to meet with all of the teachers in a day and see the gains students are making and how we can work together to improve the data even more.

—Hope Strasser

Teaching and Learning Coach

I've been working for 17 years in special education and special programs, and in doing so I know what it's like to be a segmented part of the educational process. Working with The Core Collaborative with a focus on the Impact Team Model has finally given our district a central focus. The work done by The Core Collaborative consultants has had a profound effect on all aspects of our district. For the first time in 17 years, I see all departments speaking a common language, from our special education programs, our English Language Learner programs, even our juvenile detention programs, everyone is speaking the same language. Positive things are happening in the way teachers are approaching their instruction, pedagogy is changing, and more best practice instructional strategies are being utilized. It used to be that the only place you could get high quality instruction was in the general

education setting, but with implementation of *The Impact Team Model*, standards based instruction is taking place in the hallways, in the special education department, it's happening all over our district and it's something I've never seen before. Teacher teams and school teams all working together toward a common goal is what anchors this work.

—**Mark Barlass**

Executive Director of Student Services and

Special Education Administrator

4. Implementation

To place students at the center for learning, we knew that we needed a scalable plan that could start in English Language Arts and that could also be replicated for other content areas in the future. It was important to emphasize that this was not a program but a process. As our focus on student-centered learning took shape, we focused on working with Impact Teams in three key areas:

1. Instructional Leadership

2. Teacher Clarity

3. Student Voice

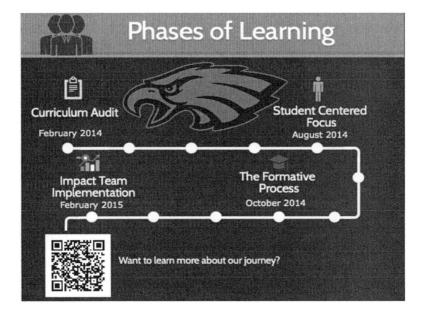

Cohorts of principals, instructional coaches, and teacher leaders developed a phased implementation plan that allowed for differentiation based on the professional learning needs at different sites while maintaining the core for Impact Teams. Implementing the formative assessment process in all classrooms would shift the environment to ensure self-regulated learning.

Over the course of 20 days throughout the school year, the cohort engaged with Dr. Bloomberg in Phase 1 of the plan, laying the foundation for the Impact Team Model by:

- Utilizing the Unpacking for Success protocol to understand and strengthen teachers' understanding of state and national standards.

This six-step protocol led to a collective understanding of the concepts and skills required for standards mastery, cognitive rigor, and using the building blocks of the learning progression for differentiation.

- Building a coherent curriculum with vertical alignment of ELA standards, including collaboratively creating standards-based rubrics that identified core competencies of each grade level.
- Using the Evidence • Analysis • Action (EAA) classroom protocol as a guide to implement the formative assessment process in classroom instruction.
- Using formative assessment evidence to refocus the PLCs on student learning using the three-step protocol EAA.
- Designing a Model Teams Approach at each school to leverage the existing expertise to effectively implement the Impact Team protocols and become a model for other teams.

In addition to face-to-face work sessions, Dr. Bloomberg spent 10 days visiting key sites and implemented the protocol evidence walks with central office administration, site principals, instructional coaches, and teacher leaders to coach leaders and teams to coach for clarity around the curriculum work.

Our leadership and administrative team have gained a much deeper understanding of teacher clarity and the formative process through leadership training on classroom walkthroughs and specific feedback to students. With a strong focus on teacher clarity, self-regulated learning, and specific feedback in communication arts from Dr. Bloomberg, we saw large percentile gains in our proficient and advanced students on state testing. Impact Teams were developed at one of our elementary schools and we saw gains in this already high-performing school. We are looking forward to taking Impact Teams and the formative process to our other schools. Paul's support was instrumental in this process and the success we have seen thus far. We look forward to the student achievement results in the future.

—Jennifer Doshier

Executive Director of Elementary Education

Finally, if the focus was on students and their learning, we needed to capture their voice. The difference between Impact Teams and other PLCs is that the protocol runs parallel to the classroom. The same conversations adults are having with each other can then be taken back to the classroom for a conference with students. When students get and give feedback around their goals, they gain confidence and clarity as well.

> We partnered with The Core Collaborative two years ago. While working with them we changed the format of our "data teams" to become more relevant and to have more of an "impact" on our student learning. These teams became our "impact teams." Through this process we were able to dig down, analyze the student data and to collaborate around strategies to impact student learning. We know much more about our students, why they are struggling, and what we can do to help them. We are able to collaborate, find specific strategies, and apply them. We have seen tremendous growth with this collaboration and are now involving students in the feedback process to continue to improve student learning. The feedback process is now reciprocal between the teachers and the students. The students have learned to goal set based off of the data they are receiving. The teachers are excited to see the growth in students and the students are excited to see the growth in themselves.
>
> —Julie Munn
>
> **Principal**

5. Lessons Learned

As with any initiative, communication is key. The ongoing challenge became effectively communicating the progress of our work and how to provide evidence that the investment was paying off for student learning to all stakeholders. The strategy that gained the most momentum was to shift perspectives by communicating celebrations, sharing models of success, and providing updates through continuous progress monitoring.

> The Impact Team in first grade is implemented to increase student reading and fluency levels plus comprehension in a variety of reading texts. First-grade teachers meet as a team weekly with data obtained on each student during guided reading group work. The students are assigned to groups based on weekly data, and teaching strategies are set for the upcoming week of instruction. Teaching becomes a true team effort with other resources such as Early Literacy teachers, peer tutors, paraprofessionals, and parent volunteers pushed in during the guided reading time.

Students are given a chance to set their individual goals, provided with strategies to achieve goals, and given their data to review. As a teacher, I am witness to an amazing transformation in education. Students know where they are in their learning, where they need to go, and strategies on how to achieve their individual goal. The most exciting part is the face of a student when a goal is reached and celebrated with a big smile! I am confident when I say that Impact Teams are responsible for the increase in the number of students meeting and exceeding reading comprehension levels in first grade.

—Karen Evans

First-Grade Teacher

A second challenge was providing adequate ongoing support for these innovations. The solution was found when we narrowed the support to those teams that were willing and stable. These model teams would then become support for new teams as we built capacity.

The work we have done with our impact team has changed the way I teach. My teaching partner and I meet regularly to norm our formative assessments as well as our summative data. We discuss not only where our students are in their learning progression and how well they understand a concept, but rather WHY they are where they are. We ask questions that help us discover why our students who have mastered a concept were able to master it, and ask what knowledge they have that others lack. Completing this step of our impact team meetings has had the greatest impact on my teaching. Before impact teams, it never occurred to me to figure out the "root cause" of student success. In the past, I had only looked at information and skills students lacked.

Together my teaching partner and I develop strategies that we implement immediately. If she sees growth in her students that I don't see in my own, we look deeper into how each of us taught our lessons and share what worked well along with what was less effective. We are able to give each other ideas to try in our classrooms. We have seen positive gains in our students' learning as well as our own.

—Brandi Landis

Third-Grade Teacher

A third lesson learned was that we needed to provide constant and consistent support to principals to enhance instructional leadership. Principals often get caught in operational whirlwinds that distract them from becoming effective instructional leaders. Keeping the Impact Team cycles going with principals allowed for the central office to remove barriers, become more efficient in allocating resources, and provide better support to the sites.

The final lesson learned was that it's necessary to continuously give and get feedback from those closest to the work—the teachers and students. As the organization became more student centered, the lens through which to make decisions became very focused, allowing for initiatives, programs, and positions not aligned to the mission to be eliminated.

> *It was amazing to me how profound the work that was done in Impact Teams changed my students' achievement. When our team really dug into the formative assessments and started asking about root causes of misconceptions, it transformed the instruction that took place in our classrooms. By pinpointing what students still needed to know, we were able to use our time so much more effectively!*
>
> **—Jennifer Sherrod**
>
> **Third Grade, Kelsey Norman Elementary**

6. Key Outcomes

District Total MSIP 5 Results (Total for all five areas)

2013	2014	2015
78.6%	85%	86.8%

District Overall Academic Results (Totals based on ELA, MATH, and SCIENCE)

2013	2014	2015
69.6%	75.9%	85.7%

District ELA Academic Results (Totals based on Proficient/Advanced+ Growth)

2013	2014	2015
56.3%	93.8%	100%

Kelsey Norman Total Results (Academics Achievement, Subgroup Achievement, and Attendance)

2013	2014	2015
88.6%	87.1%	100%

Kelsey Norman Overall Academic Results

2013	2014	2015
85%	85%	100%

Kelsey Norman ELA Proficiency Results (Students scoring proficient and advanced)

2013	2014	2015
54.1%	61.7%	78.2%

Dr. Norm Ridder, superintendent of the Joplin School District, explained district progress on state assessment results using the Impact Team Model

Joplin showed improvement for the third consecutive year, earning 86.8 percent of the total possible points in 2015, as compared with 78.6 percent of total points in 2013 on the state's school improvement formula. [The percentage of points earned is based on five key areas: academic achievement, subgroup academic achievement, college and career readiness, attendance, and graduation rate.]

"We can rest assured that we are seeing improvement, and now it's just strengthening that, and it's going to be exciting to see where we go from here," interim Superintendent Norm Ridder said.

"Much of that improvement was because of a boost in Joplin's academic achievement scores," Ridder said. The district earned 48 out of 56 total

possible points in that category in 2015, up from 42.5 points in 2014 and 39 points in 2013.

Ridder said an initiative (around self-regulated learning) implemented during the 2014–2015 academic year, before his arrival as interim superintendent, has helped bolster the district's academics. The initiative requires that students take ownership of their learning, that teachers collaborate with others in their grade level and that educators engage in a constant loop of feedback with their pupils.

He also said teachers have ramped up their reading and guided reading programs and has strengthened the relationship between their writing and reading programs for students.

"Teachers are doing a great job," he said. "It's the collaboration and raising the bar as far as expectations."

—Dr. Norm Ridder

Interim Superintendent

(As quoted by Emily Younker in
***The Joplin Globe*, October 23, 2015.)**

7. Next Steps

In 2015, the Joplin school district being guided by a new super-intendent, Dr. Norm Ridder, went through a human-centered design plan to gather stakeholder voice and create a 5-year strategic plan complete with a new mission and vision. With the help of community members, administration, teachers, parents, and students, the vision of Joplin Schools is to engage a community of learners through integrity, empowerment, and opportunity.

The plan has three main goals:

Goal 1: Joplin Schools will prepare every learner to be physically, socially, and intellectually ready to take on the challenges in the next level of learning.

Goal 2: Joplin Schools will be a team of empowered adults who are student-focused through their actions, resources, and continuous improvement cycles.

Goal 3: Joplin Schools will be a customer-focused culture that demonstrates responsible management in a purposeful manner to add value to the system for the benefit of students, staff, and patrons of the district.

To achieve these goals, Joplin Schools will build a high performing community of learners engaged in their future through a culture of continuous improvement. The next step is to continue to build capacity within the system by developing models of success and providing feedback through the Impact Team process.

Taking the classroom model approach, a repeatable 7-week plan to support schools has been created in continuing to roll out student-centered learning one team at a time.

LYONS TOWNSHIP HIGH SCHOOL DISTRICT 204

In 1888, Lyons Township High School District 204 (LTHS) was founded in the suburbs of LaGrange and Western Springs, Illinois, 16 miles southwest of downtown Chicago. Spanning across two campuses, the one high school district presently educates over 4,000 high school students from the communities of Brookfield, Burr Ridge, Countryside, Hodgkins, LaGrange, LaGrange Highlands, LaGrange Park, McCook, Western Springs, and Willow Springs. Dedicated to affirming the school's century-old motto, *Vita Plena* ("The quest for the fulfilling life"), Lyons Township High School is proud to offer its students over 300 courses and opportunities including (but not limited to) 26 Advanced Placement courses, 9 dual credit courses, 6 language programs, an automotive program, Cisco Networking Certification, Deep Diving Certification, and pilot licensure.

4000+ Students

- 74% White
- 18% Hispanic
- 4% Black
- 4% Other

16%

Low Income

11%

Special Education

3%

English Learners

24.3

Average ACT

THE CONTEXT

During the 2009–2010 school year, the staff of Lyons Township High School established professional learning communities (PLCs) in an effort to ensure all students were learning more. Following the work of Rick and Rebecca DuFour, PLCs attempt to answer the questions:

1. What should all students know and be able to do?

2. How will we know when all students have learned?

3. What will we do when a student hasn't learned?

4. What will we do when a student has learned or reached proficiency?

However, when confronted with changing state standards and assessments, a deeply rooted system of course leveling, and a traditionally private teaching culture, collaboratively answering these questions proved to be problematic for LTHS's PLCs. The four PLC questions did not provide an efficient protocol or structure for scaling up collaborative inquiry across LTHS. In addition, it was important to the leadership at LTHS that we had a focus on developing assessment capable learners. We wanted our students to be independent learners who could self-regulate.

CURRICULAR WORK: AN EASY PLACE TO GET STUCK

For 4 years, teams worked diligently identifying their course level Enduring Understandings/Big Ideas and content-based Essential Outcomes/Learning Intentions, and designing common summative assessments aligned to course-level Essential Outcomes. Biweekly PLC meetings were consumed with curricular work. As membership on the PLCs changed annually with new teaching schedules, curricular work was often repeated to incorporate the voice of new PLC members. While staff was making every effort to answer Questions 1 and 2 (as listed above), conversations were predominantly focused on teaching as opposed to student learning.

"My PLC has struggled with balancing the work load of what the district is asking us to do vs. what PLCs are actually supposed to do. With my time working with the Bloomberg team, I have realized that we should be analyzing student learning, discussing success criteria, looking at where our students struggle and why, and using this information to inform our instruction."

—Bridget McGuire

Math Teacher

A NEW PLAN

To effectively shift the conversation from teaching to learning, we needed to:

- identify that with which all students must demonstrate proficiency, prior to completing a particular course (regardless of the level of the course);
- establish common formative assessments as opposed to summative assessments;
- conduct meaningful and focused conversations around student performance during the units of instruction;
- conclude PLC meetings with an instructional action plan to implement prior to the next team meeting; and
- facilitate structured follow-up conversations to determine where students were performing after the instructional action plans were implemented.

GETTING BACK ON TRACK

Step 1: Identify the Common Denominator

To move forward, we identified the common denominator concerning student academic expectations. The Illinois State Standards (an adapted version of the Common Core State Standards [CCSS]) clearly articulate student English, math, and disciplinary literacy expectations at each grade level. Relying on state and national standards alleviates internal disputes and places the focus on the academic skills with which all students in a grade level are expected to demonstrate proficiency.

Step 2: Establish a Job-Embedded Professional Learning Plan with Articulated Outcomes

When developing a professional learning plan, LTHS consulted studies on adult learning. Studies conducted by Learning Forward, Jim Knight, and Doug Reeves concluded high-quality professional learning is aligned to state standards and local goals, facilitated frequently in teams as part of an ongoing learning cycle, and involves goal-setting, action planning, and the application of research-based instructional strategies.

As a result of the research, LTHS developed a professional learning plan that allowed 10 teams and an administrative team to meet with an external consultant six times throughout the course of the school year. While the work, during the first year, continued to be curricular, it was

AUGUST 12, 13	All 10 Teams				
OCTOBER 20		**OCTOBER 21**		**OCTOBER 23**	
Periods 1 & 2	English II	Period 1	Geometry	Periods 1 & 2	World History
Periods 3 &4/5	English III	Period 2 & 3	Health	Periods 3 & 4/5	U.S. History
Periods 7/8 & 9	Algebra	Period 4/5 & 6/7	Biology	Periods 7/8 & 9	Consumer Education
Period 10	Geometry	Period 9 &19	Chemistry	Period 10	Planning Period with Administrators
JANUARY 20		**JANUARY 21**		**JANUARY 22**	
Periods 1 & 2	English III	Period 1	Health	Periods 1 & 2	U.S. History
Periods 3 & 4/5	Algebra	Period 2 & 3	Biology	Periods 3 & 4/5	Consumer Education
Periods 7/8 & 9	Geometry	Period 4/5 & 6/7	Chemistry	Periods 7/8 & 9	English II
Periods 10	Health	Period 9 & 10	World History	Periods 10	Planning Period with Administrators
MARCH 25		**MARCH 26**		**MARCH 27**	
Periods 1 & 2	Algebra	Period 1	Biology	Periods. I & 2	Consumer Education
Periods 3 & 4/5	Geometry	Period 2 & 3	Chemistry	Periods 3 & 4/5	English II
Periods 7/8 &9	Health	Period 4/5 & 6/7	World History	Periods 7/8 & 9	English III
Period 10	Biology	Period 9 & 10	U.S. History	Period 10	Planning Period with Administrators
MAY 11		**MAY 12**		**MAY 13**	
Periods 1. 2	Geometry	Period 1	Chemistry	Periods 1 & 2	English II
Periods 3 & 4/5	Health	Period 2 & 3	World History	Periods 3 & 4/5	English III
Periods 7/8 & 9	Biology	Period 4/5 & 6/7	US. History	Periods 7/8 & 9	Algebra
Periods 10	Chemistry	Period 9 & 10	Consumer Education	Period 10	Planning Period with Administrators
June 3, June 4	All 10 Teams				

aligned to the CCSS, skill-based, formative, and common for all levels of the course.

By the end of the first year, all involved teams:

- aligned their course curriculum (map) and Essential Outcomes/Learning Intentions to the CCSS;
- developed common formative assessments concerning transferrable skills aligned to specific CCSS;
- developed a common summative assessment aligned to specific CCSS; and
- selected and implemented research-based instructional literacy strategies to use when teaching course Essential Outcomes and the literacy-based CCSS.

Step 3: Target Teams and Invite Participants

2014-2015: Targeted Teams	
Department	**Team**
Language Arts	English II
	English III
Math	Algebra
	Geometry
Physical Welfare	Health
Science	Biology
Social Studies	Consumer
	Economics
	U.S. History
	World History

To provide teams with appropriate levels of support, LTHS had to focus the professional learning efforts on a limited number of teams. The 10 courses that establish foundational skills and impact the greatest number of students early on in their high school career were targeted to be the first teams that would receive support. A staff member from each level of the course (prep, accel, honors) was asked to participate on the team, as well as the special education cross-categorical teacher and a literacy team member. This structure allowed for a smaller subset of the course teachers to set equitable expectations for students in the course.

Step 4: Locate the Right Help

The work that LTHS needed to do involved literacy, common core alignment, and assessment development and would eventually involve team structure and dynamics. To find a well-rounded consultant, we contacted Corwin and were put in touch with Dr. Paul Bloomberg. To ensure Dr. Bloomberg had the appropriate expertise and an ability to establish and expand relational trust personality across our school, we invited him to facilitate a workshop before signing a year-long contract. It was important to LTHS that we found a consultant who could maintain a focus on the formative assessment process, which we had begun to study in 2012. We wanted to continue this process through the lens of CCSS implementation because of its impact on student learning.

Step 5: Ask for Feedback and Invite Continued Participation

After one year of work with Dr. Bloomberg, all 10 teams achieved the curricular outcomes. These curricular outcomes had to be met before the conversation could shift to what students were learning. Before embarking on a second year of targeted professional learning, all 10 teams were consulted about the next steps and all team members were asked to continue. For LTHS, 96% of the staff volunteered to continue. The two staff members opting not to continue were replaced with two of their coworkers.

IMPACT TEAMS: A SIMPLE STRUCTURE TO REFOCUS PLCS

To develop assessment-capable learners, paradigm shift had to occur at LTHS; we had to refocus our existing PLC structure. Educators had to abandon their traditional teacher talk concerning what they were teaching, and had to begin to discuss was being learned and how it was being learned by their students. The leadership at LTHS desired traditionally private teachers to publically share their craft and meaningfully discuss their students' performance; they had to be provided continual support and be provided an efficient structure to learn together, resulting in the development of professional capital. LTHS discovered this support and structure in the IMPACT Team Model.

IMPACT Teams are teams of educators that collaborate on behalf of students. For LTHS, the 10 targeted teams that worked with Dr. Bloomberg in 2014–2015 to develop rigorous formative assessments aligned to the Common Core transitioned to IMPACT Teams in 2015–2016. Together, the educators on these teams are building their professional capacity by scaling up their expertise. Through the use of seven protocols, they are operationalizing the formative practices that yield the highest rates of learning.

LTHS's 10 teams are currently focusing on implementing the EAA protocol with fidelity. This is a three-phase protocol that has provided a framework to our teams to have a meaningful discussion centered on student learning demonstrated through a formative task. The protocol begins with team members sorting student work into the quality levels identified by the rubric, which is associated with their performance task. For each level of work, the team:

- examines the evidence by asking: What success criteria were the students able to achieve? What criteria do they still need to demonstrate in order to achieve the next level of proficiency?;
- analyzes the evidence by determining what skills and abilities allowed the students to demonstrate proficiency, and what skills and proficiencies potentially prohibited the students from reaching the next quality level; and
- creates an action plan (relevant to the needs of each quality level) to implement by their next meeting.

When implementing this protocol, team members leave their meeting with a plan that is instructionally differentiated. The next time they meet, they engage in the Check-In Protocol to ensure student growth is being achieved or they engage in the Microteaching Protocol as a means of learning an instructional practice focused on the formative assessment process and implemented by one of their team members.

BUILDING CAPACITY: THE MODEL TEAMS APPROACH

TIMELINE FOR BUILDINGING PROFESSIONAL CAPACITY: Evidence-Analysis-Action Protocol		
Quarter	Facilitator	Coach (Providing Feedback to the Facilitator)
Qtr. 1	Consultant	NA
Qtr. 2	Principal *or* Department Chair	Consultant
Qtr. 3	Teacher 1	Consultant
Qtr. 4	Teacher 2	Principal *or* Department Chair

At LTHS, we wanted Impact Teams to consistently focus conversations on student learning. To guarantee this end, our team members are participating in a gradual release model (the Model Teams Approach) with our consultant, Dr. Bloomberg. During the first academic quarter, Dr. Bloomberg facilitated the Evidence • Analysis • Action Protocol with each Impact Team. During the second quarter, the principal or a division chair facilitated this protocol with each IMPACT Team. Dr. Bloomberg provided on-the-spot coaching to our administrative facilitators. By providing effective feedback and job coaching, the expertise of the consultant was scaled out to LTHS administrators. During the third quarter, a teacher from the IMPACT Team facilitated the protocol with coaching from the consultant. During the fourth quarter, a second teacher from the IMPACT Team facilitated the protocol with coaching from the division chair or principal, who was receiving feedback on coaching from the consultant.

> *"This Evidence-Analysis-Action Protocol gives us a process to look at student work, analyze, and take action on how we will go about helping our students achieve the skill or target of our focus. So often our PLCs are given a directive for what to accomplish and the ultimate goal has always been to get to analyzing student work but the HOW we do that has been missing. The Evidence-Analysis-Action Protocol provides that plan and structure so that real progress and teaching can take place."*
>
> **—Virginia Condon**
>
> **English Teacher**

By providing education, opportunity for practice, effective feedback, and additional opportunity to apply the feedback to their practice, the 10 teams have been thoroughly supported in implementing this protocol. They not only understand the purpose of their IMPACT Team meetings, but also have demonstrated that they can collectively carry these meetings out on behalf of students.

NEXT STEPS

After intense practice with the EAA Protocol, the team members, who have worked with the consultant for the last 2 years, will collaborate with an assigned administrator to teach their larger course team the protocol. They will apply this protocol quarterly throughout the 2016–2017 school year, thereby

2016-2017: New Teams	
Department	**Team**
Fine Arts	Spanish I
	Spanish II
Language Arts	English I IPC
Math	Algebra II
Science	Physics
Social Studies	Psychology
Special Education	PSD
IMPACT Team focusing on new protocols	
Science	Chemistry
Social Science	World History

facilitating a structured conversation around student learning that results in a differentiated instructional action plan.

During the 2016–2017 school year, LTHS will begin the process again with eight new targeted teams. During their initial year of work with the consultant, they will align their curriculum to the Common Core, develop aligned and appropriately rigorous formative and summative assessments, and select and implement research-based instructional practices.

Finally, LTHS will support continued work with two current IMPACT Teams. These teams will spend the year learning and applying four additional protocols with Dr. Bloomberg: Calibration/Collaborative Scoring, Lesson Study, and Evidence Walks, and Microteaching. The two Model Teams will then serve as internal experts, who will be able to teach these remaining protocols to all teams in the future.

"Every successful initiative that I have been a part of during my 13 years as a school leader has involved a methodical and gradual approach to implementation. In approximately six months, we have evolved from the beginning stages of learning the Impact Team model (and associated protocols) with Dr. Bloomberg, to now having 15 LTHS faculty members from a variety of content areas who can effectively facilitate the Evidence-Analysis-Action protocol. Utilizing a gradual release approach, we will be able to have 8 self-sustaining Impact Teams during the 2016–17 school year, which will continue to build capacity with the model and protocols as we move forward at LTHS."

—Dr. Brian Waterman

Principal

REEDS SPRING SCHOOL DISTRICT

1. The Context: About the District

Reeds Spring School District (RSSD) is a small rural district located in southwest Missouri that serves five separate communities: Reeds Spring, Cape Fair, Branson West, Indian Point, and Kimberling City. It is near the tourism destination of Branson, thus there is a level of transiency present with approximately 40% of students in each grade level cohort moving over time. The district's free and reduced lunch population is 62% districtwide. The district is composed of five schools— one high school (Grades 9–12), one middle school (Grades 7 and 8), one intermediate school (Grades 5 and 6), one elementary school (Grades 2–4), one primary school (Grades PreK–1)—and a career education center that serves area school districts as well as Reeds Spring students. The teaching population is composed of primarily white, middle-class teachers.

2. Demographics

- Number of teachers: 160
- Number of students: 1,730
- Percentage of students on free/reduced lunch: 61.8%
- Percentage of white students: 93%
- Percentage of limited education students: 11%

3. The Challenge

Reeds Spring School District had been implementing professional learning communities (PLCs) for 10 years; however, the effective use of data to respond to student learning needs was not occurring districtwide. Although there were pockets of competent teams, overall the district was not seeing the impact they wanted or needed. The teams were heavily focused on the teaching (planning) and not student learning. The conversations were around looking at summative data (autopsies) and not analyzing formative evidence of student learning (health checks). Some principals added a data analysis piece to the PLC form, but even then the conversations were more on what teachers were doing and not on what students were learning.

The district has been quite methodical over the past decade with introducing initiatives to provide the needed support and professional learning to ensure proper implementation. A few of the initiatives introduced over the past several years to improve teaching and learning include a 1:1 digital conversion, Marzano's standards-based teaching and learning, implementation of rigorous curriculum such as Eureka Math in PreK through Algebra I at the high school, as well as Expeditionary Learning third through eighth grade.

Student achievement scores have generally fluctuated across the grade levels, and the free and reduced lunch population, as well as the students with special needs, have not progressed adequately. From the perspective of the assistant superintendent, Dr. Chris Templeton, Reeds Spring educators needed to learn how to collaborate productively to move teams to strategic action to address diverse learning needs. The "middle" was being served, but any learning needs outside of that were not being addressed effectively across the district. To better meet the needs of the more diverse learning groups, Dr. Templeton believed the district needed a systematic process that was timely and responsive to address the multiple learning needs for both the struggling learners as well as the higher achieving students.

In the spring of 2015, a nearby district, Joplin, offered a training on how teams use the formative assessment process to improve learning. Dr. Templeton attended the workshop and immediately realized that what she was learning was the missing piece for the Reeds Spring teams. "It struck me that this was a simple straightforward process that teams could use to look at current evidence of student learning and take immediate action to move all students forward."

This process, called Impact Teams, provided the needed protocols for teams to look at data and other relevant evidence in a deep and meaningful way and most important, to follow up strategically in the classroom. At the workshop presented by Paul Bloomberg and Barb Pitchford, Dr. Templeton connected with Paul and Barb to develop a plan for professional learning around the Impact Team process for the RSSD.

4. Desired Outcomes

Dr. Templeton identified two complementary sets of goals:

- Short-term: to refocus the traditional PLC teaming process on analyzing quality evidence of student learning to then monitor progress, and to train teams on more effective collaborative practices
- Long-term: to create a robust learning culture districtwide by:
  - Developing a collaborative culture in which teachers and leaders share and build knowledge and skills together

o Developing student and teacher partnerships in learning in all classrooms—visibly and actively sharing the learning intentions (targets), success criteria, and pathways for learning
o Creating a safe environment for feedback
o Making quality feedback ubiquitous and from multiple sources (self, peer, teacher)
o Planning for ways to strengthen student, teacher, and collective efficacy districtwide

Dr. Templeton noted that as soon as she shared the information from Joplin with the team of administrators in the spring of 2015, they were all on board with the Impact Team process, invested in revitalizing their school teams.

After the initial training with Barb Pitchford in May 2015, the building teams were ready to begin utilizing a focused protocol to guide their work. Dr. Templeton states, "Watching the increasingly deep and clear understanding of the standards as a result of the Impact Team process has been eye-opening for everyone. We thought we held common understandings of the standards but we learned we sometimes had very different interpretations of the learning expectations! The focus this process brings is unparalleled. We are seeing immediate gains in student learning as teachers and students are now clear about learning intentions and success criteria. Additionally, the teachers are very targeted in their efforts to move students to the next level of learning."

5. Implementation

Chronology—road map of professional learning:

- March 2015: Dr. Templeton visited nearby district (Joplin)
- April 2015: Took teams (two teams, each with six educators and Dr. Templeton) to visit Joplin to observe the Impact Team process
- May 2015: First District training on Impact Teams with selected teams from the five schools facilitated by Barb Pitchford. Focus: Introduction to the Impact Team process, including the team protocols and the student-centered classroom assessment process
- Summer 2015: Dr. Templeton and Barb Pitchford developed a plan for the Model Teams Approach identifying RSSD's needs, desired outcomes, and available resources
- 2015–2016 School Year: Implemented the Model Teams Approach: Focus on using the gradual release of responsibility process to develop teacher and building leaders' proficiency in facilitating the

Impact Team process. One interested (willing) team per school, the instructional coach, and the principal participate in the three coaching sessions for the year.

- o *Note:* "pilot teams" were first grade, third grade, sixth grade ELA, MS Science, HS ELA

- October 2015: Two areas of focus: (1) the EAA protocol, (3-step process that is used in the Impact Team meeting and in the classroom for student-centered assessment), and (2) the Unpacking protocol, teaching and practicing how to develop learning intentions and success criteria for teachers and students to use for self- and peer assessment.
- January 2016: Coaching/Modeling the Impact Team meeting process (EAA protocol) using the evidence from the formative assessment process. Emphasis on engaging students in using feedback from self- and peer assessment.
- April 2016: Peer Facilitator/instructional coach and/or principal and Barb differentiate by building on next learning steps:

  - o Evidence walks (protocol)—looking for evidence of teacher clarity and self- and peer assessment
  - o Principal and/or instructional coach uses the three-step EAA protocol to analyze student work
  - o Teams continue to work on teacher clarity—use the Unpacking protocol to develop success criteria for upcoming units of study

6. Key Outcomes

Reflecting on the Impact Team implementation of the past year and new practices, Dr. Templeton identified the following key outcomes:

1. Leadership is critical to the change process: It became evident that the active role of the principal promoting and participating with the model team was key to effective implementation. The buildings in which the principal actively engaged in the learning process *with* the teams, in which she encouraged other teachers and teams to observe, inquire, and "try out" the process, were the schools where the Impact Team process took hold. These were the schools where student engagement in self and peer assessment became increasingly prevalent.

2. Classroom clarity is the foundation: Discovering that teacher clarity is the essential first step to effective learning teams was an

"ah-ha!" moment for the principals and the teams. Taking time to deeply understand and agree on the expectations of the standards was the foundation that allowed the teams to develop crystal clear clarity for themselves and their students, to build effective assessment tasks, and to build a feedback culture in their classrooms.

> *"Being part of the Impact Team process influenced my team of teachers and me beyond my expectations. It became very clear to us the importance of developing teacher clarity around our priority standards and proficiency scales. We soon discovered that we would need to have tough conversations around these standards and become consistent with our expectations before we could even begin to give the students the necessary feedback to become successful learners. It has changed the way we do business at Reeds Spring Intermediate and has given us the vision for the next steps that have to be implemented to truly make a difference for our students."*
>
> **—Jodi Gronvold**
>
> **Intermediate School Principal**

3. Developing collaborative cultures: The Model Teams Approach provided models for other teams in how to effectively collaborate around developing assessment capable learners and how to have an efficient focused meeting that resulted in high-impact actions. With this two-prong focus, teachers strengthened their individual and collective knowledge and skills in areas such as peer feedback, developing and using success criteria, self-assessment, collaborative inquiry using strategic protocols, and understanding what quality evidence is. They learned to enjoy the challenges of learning together.

4. It works! Once teams began the process of building clarity and focusing on developing assessment-capable (peer and self-assessment) learners, other teachers and teams became interested and inquired about the process, some outside of the model teams, and tried it on for size. It spread organically because it accelerated student learning.

"I can remember when we first started the Impact Team training. At that point I was just hoping for something to help make our grade level meetings more effective and something to help put the focus on data-driven instruction. This process has provided so much more. Putting the focus on student learning, targeting instruction to improve results, creating success criteria, and increasing the amounts of student self-assessment has been extremely beneficial and resulted in increased student achievement as well as teacher clarity around grade level standards and learning processes."

—Laura Weber, Principal

Reeds Spring Elementary, Missouri

7. Changes and Positive Outcomes

- Teams focus on specific learning behaviors and actions, not just what they plan to teach or what they taught.
- There is increased teacher clarity and agreement of learning goals and expectations based on the focus standards. The result is a greater depth of learning for both teachers and students.
- Co-constructing success criteria with students resulted in students understanding where they are going (learning goals), where they are in the process of learning (formative assessment and feedback), and what the next steps are in their learning. "A very positive outcome. Kids are clearer and know what they need to do to move to the next level"—sixth-grade math team
- "Even struggling kids feel successful. They feel more empowered"— sixth-grade ELA team
- "We are already seeing gains in moving learners more quickly to the next level of learning in relation to their SMART goals."— third-grade team

Normagene Reid, Sixth-Grade ELA teacher, states,

"Learning to build success criteria for a performance skill in my English Language Arts classroom has been the most meaningful and useful classroom tool I've come across in a long time. I feel more in control with the success criteria in hand. The Impact Team meeting can flow easily because we can clearly discuss breakdowns in a group of students' processes and get right to the brainstorming of possible solutions and lesson ideas to keep the students moving along in a positive trajectory."

8. Lessons Learned

- The more engaged the administrators are, the deeper and more effective the implementation. We need to create multiple and ongoing opportunities for principals to learn and lead the work.
- Before we begin the meeting process, we need to audit the teams' assessments to see where they are in the foundational standards work of unpacking to develop learning intentions and success criteria. Based on what we see as a result of the audit, we need to work with the team to ensure their evidence (student work) is aligned to the standard. If they don't have rubric-bound assessments aligned to the standard, we need to work with the coaches to do that work first.

9. Next Steps (2016–2017)

1. Expand the Impact Team process to other teams (grade levels and departments). Use the Model Teams that have been trained at each school to move the practice to other interested teams. Work with the principals to determine which teams, when, and how (consider the Adopt approach).

2. Deepen the process at the secondary level. Focus on supporting the English Dept. at the High School and the Science team at the Middle School to become proficient at the process.

3. Increase the number of peer facilitators.

4. Introduce the other protocols (5) to the Model Teams.

5. We need to move the teams to more robust transferable goals/ standards that all teams can focus on (e.g., informative writing, claims/evidence/reasoning, theme/main idea, etc.).

Summary (Dr. Templeton): There has been significant growth in student achievement in the specific areas of focus for three of the Model Impact Teams (see above). They attribute the growth to:

- Much improved teacher agreement and clarity based on the focus standards, which leads to clarity of success criteria for the students
- Team focus on the three-step protocol, Evidence • Analysis • Action
- Improving professional collaboration to effectively learn from and with each other using specific protocols
- Focusing on learning the formative process in the classroom—self- and peer assessment, goal setting, using feedback not to evaluate but to learn!

"Impact Teams have broadened the focus to teacher action on a much deeper level. These meetings have created real dialogue about what we are doing and not doing as teachers. We have been able to develop better proficiency scales, success criteria, and a deeper understanding of how teacher clarity plays a huge role in helping students understand how they are progressing as learners and become successful."

—Tonya Baker

Intermediate School Instruction Coach

References and Further Reading

Ainsworh, L. (2011). *Rigorous curriculum design*. Englewood, CO: Lead + Learn Press.

Bandura, A. (1977). Self-efficacy: Toward a unifying theory of behavioral change. *Psychological Review, 84*, 191–215.

Bandura, A. (1994). Self-efficacy. In V. S. Ramachaudran (Ed.), *Encyclopedia of human behavior* (Vol. 4, pp. 71–81). New York, NY: Academic Press.

Bandura, A. (1997). *Self-efficacy: The exercise of control*. New York, NY: W. H. Freeman and Company.

Bandura, A. (2000). *Exercise of human agency through collective efficacy*. Stanford, CA: Department of Psychology, Stanford University.

Barber, M. (2011). *Deliverology 101*. Thousand Oaks, CA: Corwin.

Barth, R. (2013). The Time is Ripe (Again). Alexandria, VA: ASCD, *Educational Leadership, 71*(2), 15.

Baumeister, R., & Vohs, K. (2007). Self-regulation, ego depletion, and motivation. *Social and Personality Psychology Compass, 1*(1), 115–128.

Black, P., & Wiliam, D. (1998). Inside the black box: Raising standards through classroom assessment. *Phi Delta Kappan, 80*(2), 139–144, 146–148.

Bryk A., & Schneider, B. (2003). Creating caring schools. *Educational Leadership, 60*(6), 40–45.

Crooks, T. (1988). The impact of classroom evaluation practices on students. *Review of Educational Research, 58*(4), 438–481.

Curwin, R. L., & Mendley, A. N. (1988). *Fair isn't equal: Seven classroom tips*. Alexandria, VA: ASCD.

DeMeester, K., & Jones, F. (2009). Formative assessment for PK–3 mathematics: A review of the literature. Retrieved from http://lsi.fsu.edu/Uploads/1/docs/Formative%20Assessment%20Lit%20Review%20FCR-STEM.pdf

Duke, N. K., & Pearson, P. (2002). *What research has to say about reading instruction* (3rd ed.). Newark, DE: International Reading Association.

Dweck, C. (2006). *Mindset: The new psychology of success*. New York, NY: Ballantine Press.

Dweck, C. (2010). Mind-sets and equitable education. *Principal Leadership, 20*, 26–29.

Edmundson, A. (2012). *Teaming: How organizations learn, innovate, and compete in the knowledge economy*. San Francisco, CA: Jossey-Bass

Eells, R. (2011). *Meta-Analysis of the relationship between collective teacher efficacy and student achievement*. Ann Arbor, MI: UMI Publishing.

English, F. (2010). *Deciding what to teach and test: Developing, aligning and leading the curriculum*. Thousand Oaks, CA: Corwin.

Fencl, H., & Scheel, K. (2005). Research and teaching: Engaging students—An examination of the effects of teaching strategies on self-efficacy and course in a nonmajors physics course. *Journal of College Science Teaching, 35*(1), 20–24.

Finnigan, K., & Daly, A. (2013). System-wide reform in districts under pressure: The role of social networks in defining, acquiring, using, and diffusing research evidence. *Journal of Educational Administration, 51*(4), 476–497.

Fullan, M. (2002). Moral purpose writ large. *School Administrator, 59*(8), 14–16.

Fullan, M. (2010). *All systems go. The change imperative for whole system reform*. Thousand Oaks, CA: Corwin.

Fullan, M., & Quinn, J. (2016). *Coherence: The right divers in action for schools, districts, and systems*. Thousand Oaks, CA: Corwin.

Gallimore, R., Emerling, B., Saunders, W., & Goldenberg, C. (2009). Moving the learning of teaching closer to practice: Teacher education implications of school-based inquiry teams. *Elementary School Journal, The Chicago Press Journals, 109*(5), 537–553.

Goddard, R. D., Hoy, W. K., & Hoy, A. W. (2000). Collective teacher efficacy: Its meaning, measure, and effect on student achievement. *American Education Research Journal, 37*(2), 479–507.

Goddard, R., Goddard, Y., Kim, E., & Miller, R. (2015). A theoretical and empirical analysis of the roles of instructional leadership, teacher collaboration, and collective efficacy beliefs in support of student learning. *American Journal of Education, 121*(4), 501–530.

Graham, J. (2016, February 26). What Google leaned from its quest to build the perfect team. *The New York Times Magazine*. Retrieved from http://www.nytimes.com/2016/02/28/magazine/what-google-learned-from-its-quest-to-build-the-perfect-team.html?_r=0

Gregory, C., Cameron, C., & Davies, A. (2011). *Self-assessment and goal setting*. Bloomington, IN: Solution Tree.

Gruenert, S., & Whitaker, T. (2015). *School culture rewired: How to define, assess, and transform it*. Alexandria, VA: ASCD.

Hargreaves, A., & Fullan, M. (2012). *Professional capital: Transforming teaching in every school*. New York, NY: Teachers College Press.

Harvey, J., & Holland, H. (2012). *The school principal as leader: Guiding schools to better teaching and learning*. New York, NY: The Wallace Foundation. Retrieved from http://bit.ly/zcvOCB

Hattie, J. (2015). High-Impact Leadership. Alexandria, VA: ASCD, *Educational Leadership, 72*(5), 36–40. Retrieved from http://bit.ly/17HMIk8

Hattie, J. A. (2009). *Visible learning: A synthesis of over 800 meta-analyses relating to achievement*. New York, NY: Routledge.

Hattie, J. A. (2012). *Visible learning for teachers: Maximizing impact on teachers*. New York, NY: Routledge.

Hattie, J. A. (2014, July). Keynote address. American Visible Learning Conference. Palos Verdes, CA: Corwin.

Hattie, J. A. (2015a). *What doesn't work in education: The politics of distraction.* New York, NY: Pearson.

Hattie, J. A. (2015b). *What works in education: The politics of collaborative expertise.* New York, NY: Pearson.

Heritage, M. (2008). *Learning progressions: Supporting instruction and formative assessment.* Washington, DC: Council of Chief State School Officers.

Heritage, M., Kim, J., Vendlinski, T. P., & Herman, J. (2009). From evidence to action: A seamless process in formative assessment? *Educational Measurement: Issues and Practice, 28*(3), 24–31.

Hoy, A. W. (2000). *Changes in teacher efficacy during the early years of teaching.* Paper presented at the Annual Meeting of the American Educational Research Association, New Orleans.

Hoy, W. K., & Sweetland, S. R., & Smith, P. (2002). Toward an organizational model of achievement in high schools: The significance of collective efficacy [Electronic version]. *Educational Administration Quarterly, 38*(1), 77–93.

Jerald, C. D. (2007). *Believing and achieving* (Issue Brief). Washington, DC: Center for Comprehensive School Reform and Improvement.

Knight, J., & Cornett, J. (n.d.). *Studying the impact on instructional coaching.* Lawrence: University of Kansas, Kansas Coaching Project at the Center of Research on Learning, and Department of Special Education.

Kotter, J. P. (1996). *Leading change.* Cambridge, MA: Harvard Business School Press.

Leana, C. (2011). The missing link in school reform. *Stanford Social Innovation Review, Fall,* 29–35.

Learning Forward. (2011). *Standards for professional learning.* Oxford, OH: Author.

Margolis, H., & McCabe, P. (2006). Improving self-efficacy and motivation: What to do, what to say. *Intervention in School and Clinic, 41*(4), 218–227.

Marzano, R. (2012). *Marzano levels of school effectiveness.* Centennial, CO: Marzano Research Laboratory.

Marzano, R. J. (2003). *What works in schools: Translating research into action.* Alexandria, VA: ASCD.

Marzano, R. J., Kendall, J. S., & Gaddy, B. B. (1999). What should students know? Local control and the debate over essential knowledge. *American School Board Journal, 186*(9), 47–48, 66–62.

Meyer, D. K., Turner, J. C., & Spencer, C. A. (1997). Challenge in a mathematics classroom: Students' motivation and strategies in project-based learning. *Elementary School Journal, 97*(5), 501–521.

Miskel, C., McDonald, D., & Bloom, S. (1983). Structural and expectancy linkages within schools and organizational effectiveness. *Educational Administration Quarterly, 19,* 49–82.

Mohr, B. J., & Watkins, J. M. (2002). *The essentials of appreciative inquiry: A roadmap for creating positive futures.* Waltham, MA: Pegasus Communications.

Moolenaar, N.M., Sleegers, P.J.C., Daly, A.J. (2011). Ties with potential: Social network structure and innovative climate in Dutch schools. *Teachers College Record, 113*(9), 1983–2017.

Nicol, D., & Macfarlane-Dick, D. (2005). *Formative assessment and self-regulated learning: A model and seven principles of good feedback practice.* London, UK: Quality Assurance Agency for Higher Education.

O'Connell, M., & Vandas, K. (2015). *Partnering with students: Building ownership of learning.* Thousand Oaks, CA: Corwin.

OECD. (2008). Ten steps to equity in education. Retrieved from http://www.oecd .org/publications/Policybriefs

Perkins, D. (2003). *King Arthur's round table: How collaborative conversations create smart organizations.* Hoboken, NJ: John, Willey & Sons.

Perkins, D. N., & Salomon, G. (1992). *Transfer of learning. Contribution to the International Encyclopedia of Education* (2nd ed.). Oxford, England: Pergamon Press.

Reeves, D. (2010). *Transforming professional development into student results.* Alexandria, VA: ASCD.

Robinson, V. (2011). *Student-centered leadership.* San Francisco, CA: Jossey-Bass.

Rolheiser, C., & Ross, J. (2000). Student self-evaluation—What do we know? *Orbit, 30*(4), 33–36.

Ronfeldt, M., Farmer, S., McQueen, K., & Grissom, J. (2015). Teacher collaboration in instructional teams and student achievement. *American Educational Research Journal, 52*(3), 475–514.

Ross, J. A. (2006). The reliability, validity, and utility of self-assessment. *Practical Assessment Research & Evaluation, 11*(10), 1–13.

Schunk, D. H., & Pajares, F. (2002). The development of academic self-efficacy. In A. Wigfield & J. Eccles (Eds.), *Development of achievement motivation.* San Diego, CA: Academic Press.

Senge, P. (1990). *The fifth discipline: The art and practice of the learning organization.* New York, NY: Doubleday.

Shafer, L. (2016). *Teaching together for change. Five factors that make teacher teams successful—And make schools stronger.* Retrieved from https://www.gse.harvard .edu/news/uk/16/02/teaching-together-change

Shaughnessy, M. (2004). An interview with Anita Woolfolk: The educational psychology of teacher efficacy. *Educational Psychology Review, 16*(2), 153–175.

Shepard, L. (2006). Classroom assessment. In R. L.Brennan (Ed.), *Educational measurement* (4th ed., pp. 623–646). Westport , CT : Praeger.

Siciliano, M. (2016). It's the quality not the quantity of ties that matters: Social networks and self-efficacy beliefs. *American Education Research Journal, 53*(2), 227–262.

Stiggins, R. (2005). From formative assessment to assessment FOR learning: A path to success in standards-based schools. *Phi Delta Kappan, 87*(4), 324–328.

Stiggins, R. (2007). Assessment through the student's eyes. *Educating the Whole Child, 64*(8), 22–26.

Stiggins, R., & Chappuis, J. (2006). What a difference a word makes. *Journal of Staff Development, 27*(1).

Tschannen-Moran, M., Hoy, A. W., Hoy, W. K. (1998). Teacher Efficacy: Its Meaning and Measure. *Review of Educational Research, 68*(2), 202–248.

Tschannen-Moran, W. K., & Hoy, M. (2003). Faculty survey, 2003. Retrieved from http://mxtsch.people.wm.edu/ResearchTools/Faculty%20Trust%20Survey .pdf

Wilhelm, T. (2013). How principals cultivate shared leadership. Alexandria, VA: ASCD, *Educational Leadership, 71*(2), 62.

Wiliam, D. (2006). Formative assessment: getting the focus right. London, England: Routledge, *Educational Assessment, 11,* 283–289.

Index

A SAGE Publishing Company

CORWIN HAS ONE MISSION: to enhance education through intentional professional learning.

We build long-term relationships with our authors, educators, clients, and associations who partner with us to develop and continuously improve the best evidence-based practices that establish and support lifelong learning.

Solutions you want. Experts you trust. Results you need.

Author Consulting

On-site professional learning with sustainable results! Let us help you design a professional learning plan to meet the unique needs of your school or district. www.corwin.com/pd

Institutes

Corwin Institutes provide collaborative learning experiences that equip your team with tools and action plans ready for immediate implementation. www.corwin.com/institutes

eCourses

Practical, flexible online professional learning designed to let you go at your own pace. www.corwin.com/ecourses

Read2Earn

Did you know you can earn graduate credit for reading this book? Find out how: www.corwin.com/read2earn

Contact an account manager at (800) 831-6640 or visit **www.corwin.com** for more information.